PRAYERS A[ND IDEAS]

FOR

HEALING SERVICES

IAN COWIE

First published 1995

ISBN 0 947988 72 6

Distributed in Australia and New Zealand by Willow Connection Pty Ltd,
Unit 7A, 3-9 Kenneth Road, Manly Vale NSW 2093.
Permission to reproduce any part of this work in Australia or New Zealand
should be sought from Willow Conncetion.

The author has asserted his right under the Copyright, Designs and Patents
Act, 1988, to be identified as the Author of this Work.

Scriptual quotations bear the author's nuances.

A catalogue record for this book is available from the British Library.

Cover picture 'Crowd IV' by Diana Ong
courtesy of Zefa Picture Library, 20 Conduit Place, London W2 1HZ

We gratefully acknowledge the contribution of

The DRUMMOND TRUST
3 Pitt Terrace, Stirling

towards the publication costs of this book.

Printed by Bell and Bain Ltd., Glasgow

In thanks for healing received in Iona
and in prayer that many others
may find healing for themselves
and learn to give healing to others,
In the Name of the Father, and of the Son
and of the Holy Spirit.

Contents

The Iona Community and healing

From its earliest days the Iona Community has had 'healing' on its agenda. George MacLeod's whole message was that the Gospel is for the *whole* person, not just for the soul. He was reacting against the jibe, heard often in those days of the Depression, that the Church preached 'pie in the sky when you die, but no bread here'. Therefore George would often stress that Jesus healed bodies and fed bodies, He did not just speak about souls.

So it was that at one of the evening services during World War II George MacLeod intimated that at a future service they would be praying for the sick by name, and inviting people to submit names. He was doing this very much on the basis of the old army saying: 'Obey first, ask questions afterwards'. The Lord said, 'Preach the Gospel, heal the sick', so George began to obey orders not knowing where it would lead.

George was astounded at the number of requests which came from that small congregation. There was very little experience to go on in those days, and handling such a list set problems. On the night, the list was so long that by the time they were half way through the names those kneeling were suffering from cramp, those sitting were dozing off, and few could keep up their concentration for so long.

Advice was needed, so in 1945 the Rev. J. Madge, an Episcopal minister from Edinburgh was invited to lead a week of healing on Iona. He shared with us the experience which the Anglican Church had gained, for the healing ministry had been developing with strength since the beginning of the century in England, keeping the medical and the spiritual aspects in balance.

The next year the Archbishop of Canterbury's missioner on healing – Godfrey Mowat – came up to Iona. He had been blinded in both eyes and lived in constant pain. There was therefore nothing glib or easy about his teaching. The week concluded with a service of healing in which the laying on of hands was offered, and this really was the beginning of our weekly services in the Abbey.

Ministers joining the Community were expected to introduce some healing activity into their congregations, and for most of us this meant forming a group which prayed regularly for the sick by name.

A liturgy from the Guild of Health was adapted for our use, and came out in a pamphlet called 'Divine Healing' published by the Iona Community. It made plain that the work of the medical profession and the prayers of the Church were all part of the same pattern.

Those of us in the Iona Community were never allowed to forget that healing and our 'political witness' could not be separated. George kept drumming into us that to pray for Mary with TB in Govan and yet not to be politically active in doing something about the appalling housing which caused the TB was inconsistent. The Gospel is for the *whole* person, and our concern must be total too.

However, it did not seem necessary in those days to make the opposite point – it is just as inconsistent to be convinced that you know the answers to the political problems of nations on the other side of the world, and yet have nothing positive to offer Mary with TB! One thinks of the man who was asked the secret of his long and happy marriage:

'Well I make all the big decisions, my wife makes the little ones.'

'What are the little ones which your wife makes?'

'Well ... how we spend our money, where we go on holiday, how we furnish our house ...'

'What are the big ones you make?'

'What to do about nuclear weapons, world poverty, ecology ...'

Sometimes we are in danger of having similar priorities to the man in the story – making much noise about 'the big issues', but failing to re-present Jesus in the Power of the Spirit to the suffering folk around us in the day-to-day life of the parish.

Our concern for healing, then, like our concern for peace and justice, is just part of our reaction to human suffering. It is how we react to the individual rather than to the political system.

We have doctors and social workers as members of the Iona Community and we see their work as a ministry in response to human suffering. Their response to people who are suffering is obvious, but their work needs to be upheld in prayer by the prayers of the Church, and we are letting them down if we are less committed on the prayerful side than they are on the medical side.

This is why we have a prayer secretary as part of the resident team on Iona. The constant stream of letters from all over the world asking for prayer, and the number of people who come to the island seeking healing at one level or another is overwhelming. We have to respond personally and prayerfully to them along with our concern for peace and justice on the wider political scale.

Of course miracles happen. Only a few days before writing this, I met a woman who had gone to one of our Tuesday night services in the Abbey to pray for a friend. She thought that somebody had turned on a heater behind her, so great was the heat on her neck. She looked round but saw no heater. She realized that a whiplash injury to her neck had been healed. However, we need not be dependent on the miraculous.

Speaking personally

This book then has its roots in my fifty years of experience within the Iona Community, for I arrived for my first visit during that week in 1945 when Mr Madge came up to Iona. It is, however, a purely personal book and is in no way a policy document on behalf of the Community.

I have served in three industrial parishes, always involving myself in the industrial and political issues as well as in healing. For the last twelve years of my ministry I worked with the Christian Fellowship of Healing (Scotland). Here I was trying to put into practice something which I had learned in the parishes – i.e. the need to provide a response to human suffering which the ordinary church does not offer. We set up a drop-in centre in Edinburgh so that there was somewhere available for people in need of healing at any level of their being.

For where can a person go in the hour of acute need? Most city churches are closed during the week when folk are about, and open on Sunday when there are few in the street. Even if they are open there is not necessarily any prayerful, pastoral help on hand. What is needed is an open door, with prayer and the sacraments available to the person in need in terms which that person can understand. To ask people with deep inner pain or in severe physical pain to come to a meeting or to a service is unrealistic. To give people in deep distress an appointment three months ahead is to mock their need. In my experience in the parish I found that this *does* happen so often when people go to the doctor for help, and are referred to a psychiatrist.

Therefore we tried to work out a *ministry of availability* rather than one based on getting people to come to services and meetings. However, we did have a regular monthly healing service and I have also been involved with healing services elsewhere. It is out of such experience that this book arises.

The wider picture

We in the Iona Community were not alone in our concern to recover the Church's ministry of healing. For instance, we were in contact with other bodies which shared our concerns such as the Churches' Council for Health and Healing in England.

This movement was originated by Archbishop William Temple just after World War II with the idea that it would bring together the medical profession and the Churches to cooperate and consult on matters of healing. We in Iona followed their line in insisting that our ministry was not in competition with the medical profession.

In fact many people as well as Christians were realizing that the mind–body relationship was more important than a mechanistic view of humanity would allow. There were many in the medical profession who believed that there was this other dimension and they called it 'psychosomatic'. The counselling movement emerged from this and many Members of the Iona Community have been involved in this field.

In the sixties, the Charismatic movement began to become part of the life of the mainstream Churches. It had previously been seen in Pentecostal Churches but it became a feature which deeply affected all Churches especially the Roman Catholic Church. It stressed the Gifts of the Holy Spirit, opening up areas beyond anything the Church had taught for a long time. It was very ecumenical to begin with, and provided a bridge with the Roman Catholic Church. It also stressed the ministry of the laity, a point which the Community had always felt to be important.

A number of us in the Iona Community were involved, although recently the more extreme versions of the movement have made this difficult. Yet healing by touch, the use of 'discernment' and the 'word of knowledge' have blessed many. The healing of memories, 'deliverance' and 'resting in the Spirit' have also found a place.

At about the same time there was a rapid growth of interest in alternative medicine especially among people who came to be known as 'New Agers'. There is a constant flow of new therapies being popularized, and psychic areas opened up which perhaps contain more dangers than are realized. This has often been an issue on Iona, for many of those interested in New Age ideas are drawn to the island. Some Community Members are attracted by this side of things too.[1]

We see then, that there is a ferment going on with regard to healing, and we need to think carefully what we are about when we wonder about The Church's ministry of healing. Failure to think through the issues would mean:

- we are missing out on God's challenge to the Church in our day;
- we are left on the sidelines of worldwide issues;
- and we could be unduly influenced by extremists, leading us either to avoid the whole subject, or else allowing ourselves to be seduced into heretical and unhealthy lines of action.

1 For further discussion see Ian Cowie, *Across the Spectrum*, Handsel Press, Edinburgh, 1994.

Healing services

Should we have healing services?

Let us come straight to the basic question – should we have healing services? It is usually assumed that healing services should be part of a healing ministry. I offer, then, some practical advice about such services and some ideas for the prayers in them. I do this with some hesitation since I have considerable reservations about healing services even though, inevitably, I often conduct them!

Permit me to explain my hesitation. I believe that the true model for Christian healing is that we are inspired and empowered through our worship and our 'discipling' to go out into the world, usually in twos and threes, to bear witness to our faith, and, as part of that, we respond to the problems of the sick and the suffering by bringing the Love of God to bear on them in whatever way is appropriate to their need. This should be part of our normal life as we go about the world on our business. Having special healing services may obscure this, our true calling, and throw us back to a reliance on professional clergy and formal approaches.

There is a real danger of healing services becoming more like a spectator sport than a 'participatory, contact sport'. However, it does seem that sometimes it is right to hold such services. To find the right approach, we need to ask ourselves some important questions which are explored in the following sections.

Are healing services biblical?

The answer must be 'no'. The healings which are reported in the Gospels and Acts tend not to take place in services, and where they do, they disrupt the worship (see Mark 1.21 and Luke 13.10). They usually take place as Jesus and His disciples move around preaching the Good News. These are crowd scenes in the open air with a very different atmosphere from a respectable Scots congregation!

What is more, the healing miracles which are reported in any detail show that Jesus used a different approach for each sufferer, in some cases taking them aside.

We are therefore not justified in thinking that we can simply invite everyone to come forward for healing, giving each person the same 'treatment', and going down the line giving the laying on of hands and a short prayer to all of them.

Some people quote St Luke's comment that 'he laid his hands on them all' (Luke 4.40) or the textually doubtful verses in Mark – 'They shall lay hands on the sick and they shall recover' (Mark 16.17-18). On the other hand, others quote the comment in Mark 6.13 that the disciples preached the Gospel and anointed the sick with oil. On the basis of these verses some people feel justified in anointing everybody who comes forward, and some in laying hands on everybody.

However, these select quotations have to be set within the whole context of healing ministry as reported in the Gospels and in Acts, in which we see that Jesus deals with each person according to his or her need, with an amazing variety of approaches, often using his hands.

Only in two cases, however, is the Greek word for laying on hands used with regard to an individual (see Mark 8.22 and Luke 13:1). He was frequently asked to do so, for instance by Jairus, for this was what healers usually did (Mark 6.23). However, while Jesus used healing touch in many ways, we only have these two examples of His actually laying on hands, and even in these two cases, it seems that it was only *part* of what He did. It is much the same with the apostles in Acts.

We should also consider the reference in James 5.14 – 'if any among you is sick, send for the elders of the church who should pray over him, having anointed him with oil in the name of the Lord'. This passage presumably refers to members of the Christian Church rather than the open healing of all comers as recorded in the Gospels and Acts. The instructions are clear: the elders of the Church are *sent for* (James does not suggest waiting around thinking that the minister ought to know!); they pray *over* the patient, and they go on to anoint with oil. No reference is made to laying on hands! It is not just a question of praying *for* the sick man – it is far more outgoing and positive. We note too that the whole question of confession seems linked with healing.

As a general rule, as far as one can see in the Gospels and in Acts, the work of healing is done in settings very different from a healing service. One cannot imagine Jesus saying, 'We will have a little service of healing at 6pm this Sabbath'!

We have to conclude that while healing is a vital part of the Gospel story, the holding of healing services is something which requires real thought and prayer. Only if we feel very strongly led should we begin to hold them.

Should every service be a healing service?

Some raise the objection that we should not have special healing services – every service should be a healing service. Perhaps they should be! There are indeed real dangers in cutting healing off from the total Gospel by having separate healing services. Healing should indeed find its place in the overall setting. Yet the agenda of a properly conducted act of public worship should reflect the whole concern of God for the whole world, and not just concern for the sick. This does not leave much time to deal with individuals!

However, I have to admit that people who raise this objection have a real point in that there are indeed aspects of a normal service which have a greater healing potential than is normally recognized. In some situations the right thing to do could well be to develop these rather than to have separate services.

Let us look at some of these aspects.

The prayer of confession

Only too often one hears prayers which are guilt inducing rather than guilt relieving. Yet if the minister really expresses the hidden pain, shame and longing in human hearts, it can be a truly healing act, leading one to feel, 'Maybe I'm a mess, but I'm a mess that is accepted and loved, with hope of being sorted out.' Most of those who lead worship could do with deeply rethinking the real needs of the congregation as expressed in the prayer of confession.

The prayer of intercession

It is normal to have some reference to the sick in the prayer of intercession, and this can be developed in many ways. There is, however, a real problem if we decide to pray for the sick by name in our regular services – who chooses the names to be mentioned? There is sometimes an obvious name to be mentioned but often there are too many possibilities. Most parish churches have long lists of geriatric members all of whom need much prayer, but to include them all each Sunday would be ridiculous. We have to be selective and keep it down to three or four people.

If it is left to the minister to choose which people to name, a number of problems arise. For example: which people to select; maintaining anonymity and avoiding gossip; and when *not* to pray for someone. For these reasons, and many others, it is best not to leave it to the minister to decide who to pray for.

Let us look at alternatives:

Silence – have a regular two-minute silence left for prayer, summed up by the minister. (It is important that people know the duration.)

Silence plus names – during the silence people can name out loud those who need prayer, avoiding stating what is wrong with them. This can be a later development from the silence.

Request slips – have slips available at the door so that people can fill them in as they enter. Bring these slips up at the offering, and either read them through or offer them all up with an omnibus prayer.

Book – have a book in which names are entered and during the service lay it on the Table. Either mention the latest names or else pray for 'all whose names are in this book'.

Board – have a board on which prayer requests can be placed and deal with this in the same way as the book.

These, then, are some of the ways in which we can develop prayers for the sick in the regular service.

Thanksgiving

If we are praying for specific people and their troubles, it is important that we also give thanks for those who are healed, and the same problems arise as with prayer requests.

The Benediction

At the end of the service, when the minister blesses the congregation, the laying on of hands is being given to the congregation as a whole. For many people this is the most important bit of the service. Something important is lost if the minister just rushes through a well-known formula. Therefore we should take great care with the benediction, choosing prayerfully which one to give. It should be given lovingly and carefully. If this has been done for some time, and people are being truly blessed, then the next step can be one of focusing the Love of God on individuals after the service. On some occasions it has been very effective to say that at the end of the service the minister and others, instead of going to the door, will remain at the Table to give God's Blessing to any who want it and to pray with them about any problem which they wish to bring to the Lord.

Anonymity

Since we are all known to God, we do not need to inform Him about the nature of the trouble! Neither is it necessary for everyone to know exactly what the trouble is. If we are one in Christ, all that is necessary is that *one* person in the congregation has a close link with the sufferer. The congregation opens itself to receive God's blessing and that *one* person acts as the channel.

Hence there is no real need for full names and details of diagnosis. In fact people may well fight shy of asking for prayer if they think that details of their illness may be given in public worship.

On the other hand, when a well-known figure in the congregation is ill, and particularly if a child is very ill, then it may be right to give the full name and basic details.

The slow build-up

Bit by bit, then, we can find ways in which we can build up the ordinary service so that it is more relevant to the problem of human suffering. The prayers of confession and of intercession, the blessing and other parts of the service could take on new meaning and power.

This long-term approach is all the more important in small communities because experience shows that where people know each other well, they are often very hesitant to come forward at healing services to be ministered to by their neighbours. It is unfortunate but understandable. Hence, in such parishes, the development of the healing ministry is best served by the long, slow build up of people who work away quietly, rather than by the healing service.

On the other hand, in a city people are often willing to come forward in a strange church in a way that they would not in their local churches.

It is worth considering carefully whether it possible that the right approach is to build up the regular worship slowly over the years rather than arranging for a specifically healing service.

Looking at the possibilities

If we still feel that a healing service might be the right thing, let us look at the possibilities.

It is important to be clear in our minds about what is meant by a healing service, and this means looking at the various types of service and the issues involved.

I am going to put before you three sets of contrasting points: high key versus low key; the individualistic versus the corporate approach; and healing versus blessing. One might see them as points on the edge of a circle, and what we are trying to decide is where the right point for us might be.

High key or low key?

In order to clarify what is meant, here are descriptions of two very different healing services, one high key, the other low key. Obviously the extreme form of either is undesirable, but an element of caricature may help us clarify our minds!

High key

This service is led by somebody with charisma, using a full range of electronic equipment. Emotional singing opens people up on a psychic level, while written and spoken testimonies of previous healings increase the level of suggestibility.

Some miracles do take place and are duly advertised under the guise of 'thanking the Lord'.

Unfortunately, many are not healed and go away depressed because they feel that they did not have enough faith. There is nobody for them to turn to for the big star has moved on to another town, and the local clergy would not understand anyway ... or so they think.

Such meetings attract people with mental illnesses and in some cases terrible damage is caused because there has been the attempt to exorcise some troubled souls who actually needed healing (we will look at this in more detail later). People suffering from manic depression tend to leave such services on a soaring 'high' only to be followed by a plunging 'low'. Mental hospitals are always busy after this type of healing service.

Low key

This is a weekly service in a side chapel followed by a cup of tea. The atmosphere is one of quiet devotion. The same dozen or so folk have been meeting for this service for many years, many of them going forward for the laying on of hands each week, year in, year out. Mind you, they would tell you that they do not know how they could have got through without this ministration.

There is a long list of names to be prayed for and many of the names have grown familiar over the years. It is hard to know when to drop people off the list.

Every now and then somebody on the prayer list or somebody receiving ministry *is* healed in a way which surprises all concerned. However, the average age of those attending is high, and there are seldom any new faces. When there are, they usually do not become regular attenders and obviously this cannot go on for ever! Yet the devotion and faithfulness is impressive.

Perhaps these two extremes, slightly caricatured, can serve as a warning, and if you analyse what is for you and what is not for you in each example, you may find your happy medium.

Some of the comments just made may lead us to query the effectiveness of healing services. Indeed some ministers steer clear of this whole ministry for fear of being ineffective.

Yet we do not query the effectiveness of Holy Communion. The Lord said, 'Do this ...' so we do it and leave the results to Him. Those of us who get involved in the ministry of healing likewise take the line 'He said, "Do this" so we do it'. The rest is between those who receive it and the Lord Himself.

Yet, however we look at it, there should be a place in the worship of the Church in which individuals can seek and receive a ministry which focuses the Love of God on their particular area of need.

Or, to put it another way, it is right to sprinkle God's garden with the gentle spray of the Gospel once a week. (Unfortunately many people come to church with spirit-proof fur coats on!) But some people *do* need a strong jet of the Living Water focused at some particular area of their lives.

It is often the lack of any such occasion on which to focus the Love of God on individuals which is the cause of many congregations being mere ineffective weekly audiences.

We must not be put off for fear that our services will not be as effective as those we read about in books. As a matter of fact, having attended services by many of the 'big names', I can say that comparatively few of those who went forward were healed, and many of the healings claimed were not as clear-cut as they were supposed to be.

So do not feel inadequate if you find that you are not producing miracles all over the place! You are not Jesus Christ. While we may seek in sincerity to express something of His Love and Power, we claim to be nothing more than a pale reflection of His Glory. Honesty, sincerity and humility – with a dash of humour – will save many from disillusionment.

If the Gospel is preached in the Power of the Spirit who is Love, if that Love is expressed in an appropriate way to each who seeks healing, then whether physical miracles occur or not, people will find God. We need to take the adventure called 'faith', to venture out not knowing where we are going, like Abraham – to walk out so that there is nothing between us and failure except the Lord Himself – and then leave the results to Him, learning from our own experiences of failing, falling and weakness.

Now we move on to the second pair of contrasting points, bringing us to the question of 'who ministers?'

The individualistic or the corporate approach?

There are those who feel strongly that this is a job for the clergy, but experience shows that God often gives His healing gifts to lay people too! In trying to work out the balance, once more we find ourselves between two very different approaches to ministry.

The individualistic approach

The first approach is that of the person who has a recognized gift of healing, a charismatic personality (not necessarily 'Charismatic'!). However, it is important to note here that the translation of 1 Cor. 12 is literally 'gifts of healings', not '*the* gift of healing' and this passage is set in the context of Paul's stress that *we* are the Body of Christ, each one with different gifts. No single person reproduces the totality of the Life of Jesus for that is the function of the whole body of the Church. Therefore no *one* person has the gift of healing for all cases.

Yet there *are* gifts and many gifts are needed to cope with the various types of trouble with which one is confronted. Therefore, while somebody may be suitably gifted to lead such a healing service, this person may not necessarily be the right person to deal with every sufferer present. Services led by gifted individuals do help many, but they place a heavy weight on the person concerned, and therefore such people have a special need to be working in the setting of a *total* ministry if they are to remain healthy. They need to be upheld by and be subject to a group which can exercise a pastoral concern for them.

If you, or somebody in the congregation appears to have a real gift for healing, be sure not to 'go public' until such a caring, ministering group has been formed.

The corporate approach

The other approach is based on the understanding that the congregation is 'the Body of Christ', and therefore healing for them is a corporate act, depending on no one person. The congregation as a whole may share in the laying on of hands, and in caring for those who seek healing.

In this case the answer to the question 'who ministers?' is 'we all do'. This is ideal in many ways, but it depends on those present being deeply one in the Spirit, loving one another as the Lord commanded us. Few congregations have this unity, this communion. However, if they do, then it is a very wonderful way of ministering, for the emphasis is entirely on the work of God, and nobody in particular gets any credit. Yet one does have to be careful, for if there are people present who have been dabbling with the occult or spiritualism, they can have a negative effect. Unfortunately this is often the case today.

Teamwork

As a halfway house between the individualistic and the corporate approaches, we have the development of teams who have been prepared by training and by prayer to minister in the service and beyond it. This keeps to the New Testament pattern of disciples going out in pairs to preach the Gospel and heal the sick, and one can extend this by giving others in the congregation a special task to uphold a specific pair during ministry.

Against the background of a minister or priest with a strong healing gift, this can be seen as delegation, whereas against the background of the corporate approach, the teams can be seen as representing the Body of the congregation.

One often finds that where a minister or priest has a particular gift, the teams will tend to share in this gift, while, on the other hand, each congregation or fellowship will tend to develop a distinctive approach.

Beware of people who claim to have a gift or to be healers but who are not prepared to take a responsible part in the total life of the Church or to be subject to the teaching and discipline of the Word of God. They may be very keen to take part and then prove very disruptive. If possible make it a condition that only those who have made a regular practice of studying the Bible together and praying together should be involved in ministry.

Healing or blessing?

This leads us to the third pair of contrasting points. Naturally we have to take into account the two approaches at which we have already looked when we think about what form the laying on of hands should take.

At one end of the spectrum is the person or the congregation in which there are obvious healing gifts with sensations of heat, vibrations, 'resting in the Spirit', 'words of knowledge' and so on. This is a real healing service.

At the other end of the spectrum is a ministry which is purely an act of concentrated love, with no strange phenomena. Every ordained person has the duty and the privilege of expressing the Love of God by word and action to those who ask. We call this blessing. It is less spectacular than healing, but no less effective in the long run.

Between the two extremes there are many shades, but the ideal situation occurs when healing and blessing are part of the same ministry, with perhaps a lay person who has a specific gift doing the healing, while the ordained person leads in prayer and gives the blessing.

Now let us look at the practicalities concerning each of these.

Healing

If the emphasis in a service is to feature the gifts of healing, we will have to take account of the fact that when sufferers come forward, those ministering will need to be free to take action according to need, and if they lay on hands it will probably be on the affected part. Also there may be happenings such as 'resting in the Spirit'. Therefore it is best to arrange for at least some privacy so that there can be no question of the curious guessing what is wrong.

We must avoid the attitude that this is something which is exciting to watch since many genuine sufferers may avoid coming forward if there is a sense of spectacle, while theatrical personalities may revel in coming forward.

Another practical point to be considered if we are actually healing is that we will probably want to take quite a time with each person and therefore it is best to have somebody available who can continue to keep the congregation prayerful and awake!

Blessing

In this case hands are usually laid on the head, and therefore it is not so necessary to know what symptom has brought the person for healing. This does not raise the same problems with regard to confidentiality. Also, each case will only take a minute or so and there is not the same problem with timing.

We must be clear about the approach we are being called to take. We have seen that in actual healing, Jesus and the apostles took many different lines of action according to the need of the person. If this is to be our line then we must arrange the service accordingly. We cannot give individual attention like that with a line of people all expecting to have the laying on of hands, and expecting to be out of the church in a short time!

On the other hand, if people come seeking God's Blessing, then we can assuredly give them whatever they are open to receive, and that may be healing, or it may be inner peace. Such a service is much more easily arranged than a healing service.

Therefore, if only for very practical reasons, we must decide which we are being called to offer. Furthermore, we must make it clear in our publicity and personal contacts which emphasis we are making.

Time to decide

Having looked at these three sets of contrasts, perhaps you are beginning to get some idea as to where your position might be. Some who had hesitated to have healing services may be considering new lines not previously considered. On the other hand, some who had assumed that healing services were the natural setting for the ministry of healing will probably be having second thoughts!

It may well be the right thing to begin a healing service but we must make sure that we have people who will share in preparation by Bible study and prayer, and we must be sure that we are ready for the follow up, for such services usually bring to our attention people who need long-term ministry.

There is no point in adding a healing service into the life of a congregation in which there is little sign of 'Jesus-life'. However, if a healing service brings into focus a healing ministry which is being worked out day by day, then it can be a real blessing to all.

Questions to ask

It is important that the minister or priest consults with others when making decisions about a healing service. Perhaps it would be a good idea to circulate this list of questions, or something like it, to all concerned before any meeting to decide.

1 What are our motives?
   - to boost our church?
   - response to a real need?
   - stirrings of the Holy Spirit?
2 Are we thinking of a one-off occasion, an occasional service or of a regular feature?
3 Are we going to aim at something high key or low key?
4 How individualistic or how corporate is it to be?
5 Is the emphasis to be healing or blessing?
6 Who is going to lay hands on people?
7 Do we have people with special gifts?

8 How can we cater for people with very different needs when they ask for help?

9 Are we going to build up teams?

10 How are we going to cope with follow up?

Taking into account the realities of the parish and the layout of the church building, we must lay the whole question before God in prayer, remembering that God is always there in the *realities*, not just in the ideals which we have in our heads.

A note of warning for ministers who have had experience in previous parishes – trying to force on one parish the ideas which worked well in another is fatal. The 'growing point' in each place is different, and that is where the Holy Spirit is at work.

If it would be a good idea in your situation to hold a wider consultation, starting further back than the previous one, here is a possible list of suggestions.

Points for discussion

1 Read Matthew 9.35-10.3

Insert the name of your street or parish in 9.35

How would Jesus look at the people he saw in your parish?

Fill the names of your group into 10.3 What does this say about your calling?

2 Do we *re-present* (present all over again) Jesus as we read about Him in that passage ?

3 Try your own local survey.

How do 'the sheep without a shepherd' see your church? (In one housing scheme a secular body took an opinion poll about what people thought about the church. A number said that it did a good job for the kids and for the old folk. Nobody saw any relevance to their day-by-day lives. Nobody thought it would really matter if the church closed.)

4　What should be the characteristics of the Church?

If one of your neighbours is sick or in trouble, what has the Church to offer beyond 'being a good neighbour'?

Assuming that you *are* a good neighbour, what have you indvidually, and as part of the Body of Christ, to offer?

5　There are many simple books on healing and on prayer these days. They look at these topics from many points of view.

What books have you read?

Which were helpful, which were not?

6　What experiences do you have of healing prayer?

7　What gifts do you see in others which might equip you to represent Jesus?

8　Where do you go from here?

Going ahead

If we decide to go ahead, then there are many questions to ask, and many practical arrangements to make.

A guest preacher?

The first question people usually ask is, 'Should we invite somebody with experience to start it off?

It is only natural, after all, when you are embarking on something new, to ask for help from somebody more experienced. Yet there are pitfalls here too!

If the guest comes along, conducts a high-powered service and departs, it may leave the local people feeling (rightly) that they could not follow on from that! There can be a negative reaction to the person who comes in, 'does his thing' and then leaves.

On the other hand, it *can* be helpful if a person with experience is asked to meet a small group of interested people in the parish. The aim would be to build up a praying fellowship which develops a common mind on healing.

Then, perhaps a year or so later, a public service could be held, led by the guest to put the whole topic on the congregation's agenda. There would then be people ready to follow up.

On occasions a whole weekend can be given to such a congregational conference. The Christian Fellowship of Healing developed a pattern of meeting local clergy, and possibly doctors, on the Friday night, having an open conference on the Saturday, and preaching in the local services on the Sunday, with possibly a healing service on the Sunday night.

The only problem here was that after the sermon in the Sunday morning service, a number of people would say, 'If we'd only known *that* was what you were saying, we would have come on Saturday.' Perhaps it would have been better to have preached in the local church *first*, and then to have had the conference.

Taking all this into consideration, the conclusion seems to be that it is most inadvisable to invite guest ministers or organizations to come and conduct services etc. without preparation and follow-up. On the other hand, such guests can give a great boost to what is already going on quietly.

The form of service

The actual form of the service requires much thought. Therefore let us now begin to think about preparing it, taking into account what we have said already.

If the people who will be coming to the service are likely to be church folk used to a certain form of service, then they may well be most relaxed in that type of service but with time for ministry at the end. However, if we are liable to draw people who are strange to the church, unused to services, and certainly unused to twenty-minute sermons, it may be wise to consider a different form such as the one suggested later in this book.

People who are ill, depressed or in pain cannot take long sessions, and they find that the normal church procedure taxes their endurance, even if 'the regulars' are at home in it!

That is why what is suggested breaks the service up into a number of short blocks each of which having Bible reading, explanation and prayer. People need to understand the logic that lies behind the service and to be able to see why we are doing what we are doing.

Hence it is best to have the order of service on a sheet in front of the congregation, with the items for singing printed out, thus avoiding hymn books.

Even if one does not accept the suggested order as it stands, it might still be wise to consider afresh what elements should go into a healing service.

Communion?

We may also wonder about having the service in the setting of a celebration of Communion. This has many possibilities, but if we are going to bring in non-Church people, who would be puzzled, or even put off by the words of Communion, then perhaps it would be better not to have the Sacrament. It is not easy for us to realize how strange and possibly even repulsive the words of the Sacrament are to people who have never had them explained.

Also we often find people at these services who belong to denominations which would not let them partake, and then the very idea of Communion is undermined. Perhaps the pointers are rather against having Communion at the actual service.

Patterns of ministry

We also have to decide *how* we are going to minister to people. There are many different ways in which ministry can be arranged in the service, so let us look at some of them now.

The Iona pattern

In Iona the corporate aspects are stressed. Those who wish to receive or to share in the ministry gather at the prayer desks, or in a circle around a cross. The first relay of sufferers kneels, the 'minister' lays on hands and says a set prayer in which all can join, while those nearest also lay on hands, and those behind them lay hands on the latter and so on, forming a whole network of prayer. In this way those who come for healing also share in giving it to others, avoiding self-centredness.

The altar rail

In Churches such as the Anglican, where people are used to coming forward for Communion, it is quite simple to invite them to come forward to receive ministry as they do to receive the Sacrament. However, where there is no such tradition, it is not so easy, especially if the church is not laid out for this.

The end seat

One can arrange that the seat at the end of each row be the place for ministry. Then, if people require ministry, they move into the end seat, and those ministering go to them.

The hot seat

Chairs can be set at various places in the building, and those ministering wait at the chairs for people to come to them. Those wishing for ministry wait for an empty chair, and then move into it, thus avoiding queues. It is as well to have at least one seat towards the back in an inconspicuous position.

Hands up

Those requiring ministry are invited to raise their hands and they will be ministered to where they sit. This is not always easy in pews, especially if there is a full house. It is wise to leave alternate rows empty if this method is used.

Congregational

Those who wish for healing indicate this in their seats, then all those around them reach out to lay hands on them and pray. The person leading the service continues to lead prayer and praise, keeping an eye open for people who need special help.

Alternatively, once all who desire healing have been reached, the person conducting the service leads in prayer over them all, thus doing away with the need for vocal prayer by the people in the congregation who are actually contacting the sufferers.

In deciding the method we intend to adopt, we must take into account the layout of the church or hall, the degree to which we feel a need for privacy and the number of people involved.

For the minister preparing the service

It is natural that when we are preparing a healing service, we are more concerned than in the case of ordinary worship that the Word of God and the words of the service should probe deeply into the human psyche. We want to bring into the Light of God old memories, sins, hurts and so on which have lain dormant and festering for years.

Yet this can go too far, and some healing services are little more than an attempt at mass psychotherapy. This can be popular but undesirable, for, after all, at the back of the majority of the troubles which people bring to such a service is *self*-centredness. Therefore such undue psychic probing can pander to the cause of the trouble, whereas what is needed is that people should be challenged to look beyond themselves, and, falling in love with God in Christ, be open to the healing inflow of the Holy Spirit.

What is essential is that a clear picture of God in Christ is presented. Most ministers are tempted, when reading a story of Our Lord's ministry, to move immediately to theological implications, reinforcing their own pet theology, and drawing morals from it. This must be resisted. It is the story which matters. 'Sir, we would see Jesus' (John 12.21) is still the cry from the hidden depths, and our theology and morals so often hide the reality of Jesus. We ministers assume that people know and understand the Gospel story which has been read, while actually people are frequently very puzzled by the strangeness of it.

Hence, in the order which I suggest, the picture of Jesus which is to dominate the service and give meaning to the whole thing, is presented early on. The response in love and praise is done best in singing. (The Charismatic movement has a correct emphasis when the importance of praise is stressed.)

Emotional and spiritual experiences

This brings us to an important subject: emotion. Any minister worth his or her salt could work up an emotional atmosphere. In fact, people can be carried away by emotion at a disco or at a football match by the same methods. Some so-called services have little more spiritual content than that! Singing hymns and songs of praise can attract many. Yet, while a right handling of emotion is indeed part of preparing a service, we must never forget that an *emotional* experience is not necessarily a *spiritual* experience. Many people make this mistake, and their religion becomes an escapist drug.

We have to remember the point made earlier that many emotionally damaged people come to a healing service, and a high emotional content can unbalance them, or at least frighten them off. (I often advise people with schizophrenia to attend low-key services, and to avoid the exciting types of service which attract them.)

Also, we must avoid arousing unhealthy feelings of guilt, realizing the difference between that awareness of one's sin which arises from fear (a bad ally) and that which arises from realizing that one is loved beyond belief and hence gladly realizing one's unworthiness (as expressed in 'Amazing Grace').

Another aspect to avoid is the 'you must have faith' line, which results in people going away feeling a failure once more. We are there as a Church to *inspire* faith, not to demand it.

On the subject of faith, we have to be clear as to the difference between credulity and faith. Believing that the Lord can heal is not faith itself but credulity. Working up credulity by quoting testimonies is dangerous, even though testimonies have a place at times. Consider the woman who believed that merely touching His Garment could heal her. Jesus was not satisfied until she had faced Him, and in that relationship credulity became a loving faith in Him (Mark 5.28).

These, then, are some of the points which ministers preparing a service should consider.

Preparation for those taking part

Before the service itself, it is important to build up the whole atmosphere of prayer. Where possible those who have been preparing the way and/or those taking part should meet in the church praying together, putting on 'the whole Armour of God' (Ephesians 6.10), and ministering to each other.

This preparation should include all those taking part, including, for instance the stewards mentioned below, the musicians, the people on the bookstall if there is one, and so on. We do not want to give the impression that there are first- and second-class grades of helpers.

In some services those who are going to lay on hands actually lay hands on each other as part of the service immediately before ministering. In one way this is good, for it makes it plain that we all need to receive and all need to give. Yet it can become exhibitionistic and ritualistic and it is perhaps better to pray for each other in privacy before the service along with all the others concerned.

Musicians, stewards and others with an active role should be fully briefed and upheld in prayer.

Stewards

It is important to have competent stewards on duty throughout the service since there may be people who are new to the church and people with problems. We must help them to feel at home in a way that the normal congregation does not need to (or does it?).

Stewards should be ready to come into the church with newcomers, to show them to a seat, and perhaps to introduce them to those who are familiar with the scene. They must also be ready to move about the church if need be during the service and not be 'tied' to the door.

Sometimes people have to leave before the end of the service, or they may become upset, or need the lavatory (are the 'Ladies' and 'Gents' clearly marked?). People with bad backs may need to have special arrangements made for seating. The steward may notice that somebody is upset and needs attention without waiting for the time of ministry. During the time of ministry it sometimes becomes evident that somebody wants ministry but cannot get themselves to the requisite place. Therefore the stewards must be alert throughout the service, and be people with initiative.

Appointments

We have mentioned cases in which more is needed than can be tackled in the course of a service. Therefore somebody with an appointment book should be available to whom people can be referred in order to arrange for further ministry. This person should be pointed out so that a person in the congregation who is too shy to come forward can make a private appointment.

Bookstall

It is wise to have a bookstall with leaflets (e.g. those from the Christian Fellowship of Healing or Renewal Servicing), and somebody with pastoral skill looking after it. I stress the importance of this having found that the person on the bookstall is often the one who makes really vital contacts after the service, having noticed which leaflets people look at. This can be an important pastoral function.

Gifts of the spirit

One area of ministry which is fraught with danger is the place given to those who manifest 'gifts of the spirit'. They can lift the whole service onto a higher level or drag it down into a jungle of psychic ego-tripping. In contrast, the ministering teams are made up of people whose dedication is proven, and the Holy Spirit may work through any of them. However, if the Spirit has given one person a gift which is good for healing physically, presumably we should call in that person if physical healing is needed. If another individual is an understanding person with the gift of Wisdom, and perhaps Knowledge, we would call in this person for somebody who needed inner healing.

The gift of 'discernment'

This is of great use in a healing service. 'Discernment' enables a person to 'see' both hidden good and evil in people. It is worth considering keeping a 'discerner' working 'free range', sitting quietly where each patient coming forward can be upheld in prayer, and in a position such that those ministering can easily call for help. If evil or darkness is discerned in somebody coming forward, the discerner should move quietly up beside those ministering.

The worst thing that can happen at this point is for those ministering to become anxious: 'Oh dear, we're in for deliverance; we'd better take on the armour of God' etc. They should be spiritually prepared already, for one thing, and for another, anything which heightens the level of anxiety or of fear in the patient must be avoided.

The conversation and sequence might go something like this:

Hello *(give name of discerner)*. It's nice to see you, have you come to help? Good.

Now *(give name of patient)*, you have turned to Jesus for help haven't you? Well Jesus has given us His Authority. *(Do not say 'over demons' or 'over evil spirits'.)* It is in His Name, with His Authority that we come to you now'.

At this point all should be looking at the patient with love, but not touching them.

Silently the ministering team should join to bind whatever evil is there and to command it to go in Jesus' Name.

A prayer of quiet praise and love might follow.

If the discerner feels that it has gone, all join to bless the patient.

However, it should be made clear to the patient that a lot of pastoral care will be needed in the near future.

If the discerner feels that the evil is still there, it suggests that the patient has in some way invited it in, and that some repentance and renunciation may be needed before cleansing can take place. Then, either the patient should be taken aside and receive a full ministry of deliverance or else the evil must be bound and a later appointment made. Then the patient can be blessed. Plans for follow-up care are essential, and those who ministered must take on the responsibility for praying regularly for the patient.

For further guidance on 'deliverance' the booklet 'The Minister and the Deliverance Ministry' by John Richards, Renewal Servicing, is very helpful.

Sometimes people think they are 'possessed' because they hear voices. If somebody comes forward hearing voices or the like, then the ministering teams should be able to look across to the discerner for a simple check. Such people usually have a mental illness and should simply receive a blessing with as much love and peace radiating as possible. Mental illnesses are somewhat more complex and need more careful treatment than the odd demon or two! It is important that those ministering do not allow themselves to get caught up with listening to lengthy stories. The emphasis must be kept upon love: 'Just be still and allow us to pour His Love over you.'

We should avoid using words such as 'possession', and try to dissuade the patient from using them too. The whole concept is fear-creating and therefore unhealthy. Furthermore, it is not Biblical, although unfortunately it appears in English translations of the Bible. The New Testament uses various phrases – 'having a spirit of uncleanness' (Mark 5.2; 7.25; Luke 4.36; 6.18; 11.24); 'in a spirit of uncleanness' (Mark 1.23); 'having a dumb spirit' (Mark 9.17); 'having a spirit of an unclean demon (Luke 4.33); 'having an evil spirit' (Luke 7.24; 8.27); 'demonized' (Mark 1.32; 5.32; Matt. 9.32; 8.25). However, the New Testament never suggests that a demon or devil can *have* us. For our use it is better to use a phrase such as 'catching a psychic infection' in the same way as we may speak of 'catching a cold'. We have to be clear that such entities cannot have or possess *us*.

This sort of issue needs to be discussed and arranged between those ministering before the service. Then all those concerned know what they are doing and can communicate with each other without words which might alarm the patient and people in the congregation.

Physical healing gifts

These are also useful 'free range'. For instance, I recently attended a service where somebody came forward with a broken ankle which would not heal. The two people ministering were wonderful on inner healing, but if there had been somebody present with the gift of physical healing, I would have called that person in.

The 'gift of knowledge'

This is very useful too. In one-to-one ministry it leads into the situation in which the patient says, 'But how did you know that?' It can also be apparent in a service but it can become a real ego-trip. If someone in the ministering team proclaims, 'There is somebody here with a bad back and the Lord wants to heal them', this can appear very impressive. It is strange, however, that people who claim to have this gift tend always to point to the same complaints, and these are complaints which one can be almost sure are present without any divine intervention! As so often happens, what began as a real gift becomes 'Mr X's thing' and he feels he has got to demonstrate it at each service. Then it goes badly wrong.

If one of the team does tend to get 'words of knowledge', then provide a note-pad on which the 'word' can be written and quietly handed to the person leading the service, who can then use the information without exhibitionism.

What if it is the minister who manifests these gifts?

Then beware! 'Gifts of healings are for the upbuilding of the Body of Christ,' as it says in Ephesians 4.12. They are not to enable an individual, minister or not, to be a healer. Ministers face special temptations here. If they slip everyone but the minister sees the ego-trip plainly, however much they verbally give the glory to the Lord.

What if someone in the congregation manifests these gifts?

Much of this applies if there is somebody in the congregation who claims to have 'gifts of healings'. Beware people who claim to have *the* gift of healing. Nobody has the power to heal all illnesses. Any healing gift, as with a musical gift or any other, must be offered up to God, and surrendered. Those who use the church as a showground for their gift cause disruption. As with the minister, such people should keep quiet until there is evidence that the gifts are being shared with others as they study the Bible and pray together. If they will not share in these gifts, then there is no place for them in the church's ministry.

As Jesus delegated and shared His Authority surprisingly early in the Gospel story, so those with individual gifts must also be concerned to delegate and share. We referred earlier to the fact that any group will tend to share in the gifts and ministry style of the minister, and this is as it should be.

If you believe you have a healing gift but no-one is expressing interest then it is important to keep healing low-profile until there is. It may be, of course, that the minister is setting such high doctrinal and moral barriers that nobody who is emotionally healthy will dare to come near. This is one way the minister can keep up the ego-trip position, blaming others for lack of faith, but perhaps gathering together a very unhealthy little clique. As Jesus delegated and shared His Authority surprisingly early in the Gospel story, so those with individual gifts must also be concerned to delegate and share.

What if no-one, including the minister, manifests these gifts?

Then it is one of two things: you are not ready to have a healing service and you must search your motives deeply to see why you feel that you should have one; or it may be that God is calling you to a real act of faith and obedience. It requires more faith to have a healing service when you are aware of no gifts than when you have proven gifts!

If God is saying, 'do this' then you do it, even if it seems stupid. Remember what I said earlier about celebrating Communion because we are told to not because we have calculated the effects. Therefore, if there are no obvious gifts yet you feel led to hold a healing service, you could begin with something which was nearer a service of blessing, and in due course it might well be that gifts would emerge.

We have looked at a number of aspects of ministry to the sick. It all boils down to something quite simple: our job is to encourage the sufferer to open up in Faith to the Love of God in Jesus Christ, and then to express His Love to them by whatever means we can. If we are doing this, humbly and obediently, building up one another in love for God and for humanity, then The Lord will equip us with such gifts of the Spirit as we need to do what He asks of us.

The 'Touching Place'[1]

Now we move on to consider the issues which arise at the focal point of the service – when people actually come to the 'touching place'.

People who come forward for healing

Those who come forward for healing fall into two categories: those who are already linked with the healing work of congregation, and those who have come to this service from outside. Let us look at each of these categories.

Regular attenders

Why do such people, who *could* receive personal ministry any time, come forward at a healing service when they cannot receive the same attention? There are at least three reasons:

- some are exhibitionists who make a habit of going forward for visiting evangelists, healers etc. It has become an attention-seeking device. When we realize that we are dealing with such behaviour, we should be short, sharp and loving, giving them an assurance of God's love and a blessing. We should give the person a Bible verse and lead into prayer, and, unless we are very sure that some particular healing is being given, we should send them firmly back to their seat.

- some feel that the sessions they attend regularly are too cosy and the sense of occasion at a healing service meets a need. This should make us think again about what happens at the times when they do come to church normally. Once again, unless we are sure that guidance or healing is being given, we should be short, sharp and loving. They can receive prolonged ministry elsewhere, and we must not use up time needed by newcomers. Listening in this case is out of place – except to God!

- occasionally some sensitive soul realizes that somebody needs to break the ice, and comes forward to prepare the way for others. They should certainly receive a blessing.

---

1   'A Touching Place' is the title of a casette by the Wild Goose Worship Group, Wild Goose Publications, 1986.

Newcomers

Those who come in from outside the church *do* need to be listened to to some extent. We have to decide whether to advise them to make an appointment (and help them to do so afterwards), to take them aside into privacy, to call in the minister immediately, or just to proceed there and then.

Counselling and healing services

In all these cases we must remember that while listening and counselling are in place on most occasions, a healing service is not the place for them. In private sessions it is natural for the conversation to be patient–symptom centred, beginning with 'what's the trouble?' and then working round to being Christ-centred.

In the service, however, we should start from being Christ-centred and remain there! For instance we may begin by asking, 'What has God been saying to you during this service?' rather than asking what is wrong.

If you feel counselling is needed, make an appointment, bless the person and send them firmly back to their seat!

To know or not to know exactly what is wrong

In some healing services the minister asks what brings the person forward while in others this is not done. The focus should not be on what's *wrong* with the patient but what is *right* for them. As we have seen, a healing service is different from a counselling session or a doctor's surgery, in that the focus is on the Love of God, not on the symptom. We are trying to point people away from themselves and their problems, not reinforce their absorption in those problems.

Therefore there is much to be said for the minister *not* being told what is wrong, for then, if the prayer is relevant in a way they could not know, the sufferer knows that it is of God. However, each person ministering must work out what is the right balance for them.

'Resting/slain in the spirit'

Sometimes people swoon and this can be mistaken for fainting. This swooning is a sort of 'spiritual anaesthetic' given when something deep has to be done and there is not time to work on the conscious mind. John Richards, in his excellent booklet mentioned earlier, prefers the term 'resting' to 'slain' since it is less sensational. While 'resting in the spirit' does happen at times, make sure that it doesn't become the focal point of the service. It is a practice which can be taken up in an exhibitionistic or hysterical way.

If someone really does 'rest in the spirit' they go down backwards whereas the person fainting tends to crumple forwards. If one is ministering to people who are in a standing position, it is wise to have a strong 'catcher' behind them. If they are sitting, then they appear to go to sleep. The person 'resting in the spirit' has a good colour and breathes easily. Someone with the 'gift of discernment' will know at once whether it is a medical condition, a hysterical exhibition, or a true act of the spirit. If you have a doctor or nurse in your midst, they too will know, and this can be a help until you are experienced enough to know for yourself. In either case tell somebody prayerful to stay beside them, ready to listen and respond lovingly to any need they express on awakening.

Proxy ministry

This occurs when somebody in the congregation comes forward to receive the laying on of hands on behalf of another who cannot be present in person.

There is no Biblical precedent for this. When people came to Jesus to seek help for somebody else, Jesus either went with them, as with Jairus' daughter (Mark 5.21), or dealt with them silently at a distance, as in the cases of the nobleman's son (John 4.46) and the centurion's servant (Luke 7.1-10). In no instance do we find Him laying hands on somebody as a proxy for somebody else. This practice seems to have arisen within the Anglican renewal of the healing ministry in the early 1900s. However, God seems to have blessed this practice by using it, so we accept it with caution.

There is a danger. It depends on a close identification of the proxy with the patient. In some cases this has led to the suffering of the patient affecting the proxy, as in the case of a woman who came forward as proxy for her depressed friend and while the friend was helped, the proxy went away with depression and had to come back. Hence the relationship should always be committed to God in a prayer.

The final point, coming back to the principle that a patient should never dictate the form of treatment, is that we have to make up our own minds as to whether to accede to the request or not. Notice how often people came to Jesus asking for the laying on of hands only to find that He did something else. I mentioned Jairus' daughter and this is a case in point. Jairus requested the laying on of hands whereas Jesus spoke the Word of authority, awakening her, and only then did he take her hand to help the sleepy girl to her feet. It was His Word not His Touch which awoke her. The decision whether to do as requested or whether to simply pray for the patient with the proxy, or even perhaps to arrange for a visit must rest with the person ministering – a prayerful, loving decision.

We should ascertain whether the proxy has the patient's authority to act in this way, and whether the patient knows of the occasion. It is important that the patient does not find this intrusive. Occasionally it may seem right to proceed even if the answer to both questions is 'no', but usually it is not.

In any case, we will not turn the person down flat; indeed we may decide that deeper action is needed, as in the cases of the blind man and the deaf-mute in Mark's Gospel (Mark 7.31-37; 8.22-26). Jesus took a lot more trouble with them than people had expected.

When praying for somebody through a proxy

Pray for the sufferer by name, lifting them up into the Presence of the Lord. Turn to the proxy to bless the sufferer by laying hands on the proxy.

e.g. In Your Name, Lord Jesus, we bless John, through this Your daughter Mary.

(To the proxy) John is in God's hands now. Let go. Christ be between you and Him. Go in peace.

Anointing

In some services everybody who comes forward is anointed, in others the oil is kept available in case of need, but in most churches there is no mention of anointing in the healing services. It is Biblical, however, and we should consider it.

In Biblical times oil was poured on people for three reasons:

- As a healing, soothing gesture. We find this in the twenty-third Psalm and in the story of the Good Samaritan who poured oil and wine into the wounds of the robbers' victim (Luke 10.30-37).
- Kings and priests were anointed to set them apart for their work.
- As an act of welcome such as a guest arriving after a long journey.

In Mark 6.13 we read that the disciples of Jesus went out preaching the Gospel and anointing people. In James 5.14 we read instructions about what to do if a member of the Christian community is ill, and this includes anointing. There is, however, no mention of Jesus anointing with oil, and neither is there any reference to the practice in Acts.

As the centuries passed by it came down to being 'the last rites', and even today if some lapsed catholic is offered anointing they will think it means that they have reached the end of the road! The Church of England began using anointing as a sacrament of healing in the early 1900s and the Roman Catholic Church followed suit after Vatican II. It is one of the sacraments in the Roman Church and the rules of that Church forbid its members to receive it from other Churches. Out of courtesy we should not try to anoint Roman Catholics. The Reformed Churches do not have any rules about the use of oil.

It is normally olive oil which is used and we consecrate it much as we consecrate the bread and wine at Communion, perhaps using the same prayer as a basis.

In a service it is best to have the oil, spoon, and a few tissues on the Communion Table, available for those who feel that a patient needs it. While we know that lay people in the early Church, and Roman Catholic laity today do anoint with oil which has already been blessed, it is perhaps wiser to call on the minister to anoint if it is lay people who are ministering.

There are two methods of anointing:

- The oil is kept in a bottle and a small spoon is set beside it. A drop of oil is placed in the spoon, and applied to the patient, either by pouring on the head or by thumb smear. Some people, including Roman Catholics, consecrate the oil in the bottle, perhaps at a special service. Others consecrate only the drop in the spoon as it is being used.
- One can buy a special little screw-top metal jar with cotton-wool in it called an oil stock. Consecrated oil is poured into the cotton-wool, so that all the ministrant has to do is to dip a thumb in and smear the oil on the patient.

There are no real guidelines as to when anointing rather than the laying-on of hands is right, and those with experience vary in their practice. My own feeling is that anointing is especially relevant if a person is going for an operation, if there is a deep need to say to somebody, 'you are special', or if the body has been violated by an accident, war, an operation which went wrong, or by sexual abuse. In these cases it should be done lovingly, with dignity and some proper sense of ritual. It is definitely more objective than the laying on of hands.

Usually we anoint the top of the person's head or their forehead, although sometimes it makes sense to anoint their hands, or even, in the case of sexual abuse, their bodies.

As in all sacraments and sacramental-type acts, the action in itself may mean little, but set in the context of proclaiming the Gospel and prayer it is a powerful means of healing. We human beings, being what we are, often need to go beyond the verbal to a physical expression of the Love of God.

Here then, are some thoughts about ministering. Think through them, and see which ring bells and which do not. Perhaps I should have written 'which the Holy Spirit lights up for you', not 'ring bells'!

Prayers for the 'Touching Place'

Any people who are organizing such a service must come to a common mind as to which of the following types of prayer they are going to use, and that, of course, depends on whether it is really a service of blessing or a truly healing service.

Prayers for blessing

The set prayer

If it is a service of blessing we would probably us a fairly formal wording. One may use the same prayer for every person coming forward. The advantage of this is that it avoids exhibitionism in the person ministering, it respects the confidence of the patient, and it emphasises the more objective working of the Holy Spirit. The disadvantage is that it gets monotonous, it does not give the individual touch which, as we have seen, is typical of Jesus, and it can appear mechanical and uncaring to those who do not understand.

It is therefore all the more vital that the set prayer should arise out of a prayerfulness just as deep as that required for spontaneous prayer. Each time it is said, it must be said with a fresh authority and love. Here, then, are some examples.

In Iona we use a version of the prayer by the late George Bennett, sometime warden of Crowhurst.

> *The Spirit of the Living God, present with us now,*
> *enter you, body mind and spirit*
> *and heal you of all that harms you.*
> *In Jesus' Name, Amen.*

The original is:

> *The healing mercies of our Risen Lord Jesus Christ,*
> *present with us now,*
> *fill your whole being, body, mind, soul and spirit*
> *and heal you.*
> *May He do away from you all that harms or hurts you,*
> *and give you his peace.*

Christopher Hamel Cooke in *Health is for God*[1] suggests:

May God who made you, make you whole,
as He would have you be,
in the Name and through the power
of the Risen and Ascended Christ,
present with us now in His Holy Spirit.
May He send you forth
renewed and restored to do His Will
to your benefit and in the service of others,
but above all to the glory of His Holy Name.

The benediction

There are a number of benedictions, trinitarian and Biblical. One can make a list of them and learn them by heart, although most ministers know them already, and say a different one over each person who comes forward. Surprisingly often people will say later: 'How did you know ...?'

One can make up blessings from well-loved Biblical passages, or use some from other sources. Here are some suggestions.

Thus saith the Lord who created you, He who formed you:
'Fear not for I have redeemed you.
I have called you by your name and you are mine.
Whatever you may pass through,
fear not for I am with you.'
Therefore go on your way in peace.
In the Name ...

Know that there is nothing in past, present or future,
nothing in life or in death,
no angel, no demon, nothing
that can separate you from the Love of God in Jesus Christ.
Therefore go on your way in peace.
In the Name ...

1 Published by Arthur James, 4 Broadway Road, Evesham, Worcs WR11 6BH

The God of peace Himself sanctify you in body, mind and soul.
Your body is the Temple of the Holy Spirit who lives in you.
Therefore go on your way in peace.
In the Name ...

The Peace of God which passes all understanding
guard your heart and mind in the knowledge and love of God
and of Jesus Christ our Risen Lord.
Therefore go on your way in peace.
In the Name ...

The Lord of Peace Himself give you peace.
Wherever you go, whatever you do, the Lord be with you.
Therefore go on your way in peace.
In the Name ...

Grace, mercy and peace, from Father, Son and Holy Spirit,
bless, heal and protect you,
this day and every day, through time and through eternity.
Therefore go on your way in peace.
In the Name ...

Into God's gracious Hands we commit you and your loved one(s).
Let not your heart be troubled, neither let it be afraid.
The Lord gives you His peace,
peace such as the world cannot give.
Therefore go on your way in peace.
In the Name ...

Know the Love of Christ for you and in you,
He does far more than we can ask or imagine
by the Power of the Holy Spirit in us.
Be filled through all your being with all the fullness of God.
Therefore go on your way in peace.
In the Name ...

The Good Shepherd Himself lead you on,
through the dark valleys of life
and through the green pastures.
His angels of Goodness and Mercy escort you,
that you may know that you are His,
through time and through eternity.
Therefore go on your way in peace.
In the Name ...

The Love of God uphold you.
The Peace of God enfold you.
The Life of Jesus heal you.
The Word of Jesus lead you.
The Fire of the Spirit purify you.
The Wind of the Spirit drive you forward.
Have no fear.
The Lord is with you, not against you,
with you to protect you in danger,
with you to correct you when you go wrong.
God is Love, Father, Son and Holy Spirit,
One in love, in love for you,
this day and all eternity.

Deep Peace of the running wave to you,
Deep Peace of the flowing air to you,
Deep Peace of the silent stars to you,
Deep Peace of the quiet earth to you,
Deep Peace of Christ, the Son of Peace to you.[1]
Therefore go on your way in peace.
In the Name ...

1 from a much longer healing invocation by Fiona Macleod

Prayers for healing

If, however, we are really going to be *healing* people, we would, as we have seen, need a different approach.

When the person comes forward get them relaxed, ask for their name and for a rough idea of what is wrong. Check if they have seen a doctor if that is appropriate. If medical treatment is involved, remember to bless it as part of the prayer.

Touch them in a friendly manner, maybe taking their hands, or putting a hand on their shoulder. If then you feel that it is right to pray for specific healing you can move on. If not bless them lovingly as in the previous section.

How does one know? People who work together do develop an understanding, and can let each other know without many words – if any! – if they feel a gift of healing is being given in a given case. Usually the sign is a heat or tingling in the hands, a warmth or a light. However, each person is different, and each pair of ministering folk must work out their own pattern and know how the Spirit works through them.

If a definite gift of healing is being given, the person ministering moves their hands to the place where it is felt most strongly, usually moving in such a way that the trouble spot is between the hands. (I have known incredibly accurate diagnosis done this way.)

One would say something like this:

'(*Give name of person*), we are doing this in the name of Jesus because the Father loves you. We claim the Power of the Spirit to heal you.' (*Keep the emotional level low.*)

Once in place, keep the hands in position for as long as you feel the power is flowing. One may wait in silence, or chat quietly in a relaxed Jesus-centred way. Some people like to ask the patient what is being felt, some prefer not to.

When the power is 'switched off' bless the person as above, and arrange to keep in touch if possible.

Some speak in tongues at this point, but I have known patients who have been so bewildered at hearing this that they have shut off, and the healing could not flow. Occasionally it has proved a blessing, but one has to be very careful.

The tailor-made prayer

The alternative to the set prayer is the tailor-made prayer which is designed to fit the specific situation. The person ministering waits for a Bible Verse or a picture of Jesus in action to come to mind, and then applies it to the sufferer with authority, ending with a blessing. For example:

In the Name of Jesus of Nazareth and in the Power of His Spirit we lay hands on you *(give name)* beloved son/daughter of God. *(silence)*

(Then say a short scriptural phrase such as one of the following.)
Be filled, through all your being with all the fullness of God.
Fear not, the Lord is with you.
Be whole, to the glory of God.
Be strengthened with might by His Spirit in your inner being.
The all-sufficient strength of God make good your weakness to His Glory.
Be cleansed by the outpouring of His Holy Spirit.

The Lord Jesus who *(here mention the healing work of Jesus which has been the theme of the service)* and who is present with us now, heal you.

Jesus is the Light of the world, and we focus that healing Light upon you now.
(Then, after a pause, a trinitarian blessing.)
Grace, mercy and peace, from Father, Son and Holy Spirit, bless, preserve and heal you. Go in peace.

A warning!

I have had some unfortunate experiences with ministers praying loudly over people, giving away confidential information. This upsets the sufferer, it panders to the inquisitive in the congregation, and leads sufferers in the congregation to think twice about coming forward!

A pattern for prayer

If we are going to take the line of using tailor-made prayer, then there are certain patterns which we need to learn, and each person ministering will tend to develop their own pattern, although each ministering congregation or group will also tend to have a common element.

Whether we lay hands on the head in blessing, or whether we are open to a more healing form, the essential thing is that one prays with the authority of love, not asking God for something, but conveying to His child that which Our Father wants to give. Any asking should have been done earlier in the service.

There is a basic discipline to be learned in public prayer. This is not to deny spontaneity, but to encourage it. Compare it with playing music, painting or driving a car. There are certain disciplines (*disciplings*) which must become so much part of you that you cease to think about them. Only then can one be spontaneous effectively.

Here, then, is the basic pattern.

– *Clarity of vision*

Prayer must spring from a clear vision of God, e.g. Father, Light of the World, the Good Shepherd or one of the stories about Jesus. These images must have been thought about and meditated upon in private many times. Then, in praying aloud, the language and phrases to be used will emerge naturally. The art of praying with people is to choose (or rather to allow the Holy Spirit to choose) the right name or word–picture of God to open the prayer, so that it opens the line, so to speak, between the person and God. Therefore we begin in silence, waiting on God for the right opening.

Metaphorically if not literally, we sit *beside* the person, on the same level, at one with them, a fellow sufferer, looking up to God.

– *In the name of the sufferer*

We then speak to God in the name of the sufferer, expressing things which perhaps the sufferer could not put into words. We express the deep need of the soul for God.

Metaphorically, if not literally, in this prayer we kneel *beside* the patient, facing God.

— *In the name of Jesus*

Now we turn to the patient and express the healing Word of God to him or her. Whatever words or actions are appropriate must emerge from the awareness that in Christ we do have the authority of love. Just adding 'in the Name of Jesus' means nothing. It is when we know that we are acting and speaking with His Authority – 'in His Name' – that things happen!

Metaphorically if not literally, at this point we stand *facing* the sufferer, representing Jesus.

This is the basic pattern, but having learned it, one is free to vary it, of course.

All this need not take long: 'Lord Jesus, help. In the Name of Jesus, be healed' is the ideal – it takes about ten seconds. Note that there is no record of Jesus speaking long prayers over people, and note the practice of the apostles in Acts. Long prayers are usually a sign of our weakness and uncertainty.

We really need to practise this in a small group before 'going public'. We would only use those whom we know to be disciplined in this way. What we want to avoid is the sort of rambling prayer which is just a stringing together of high sounding religious phrases mixed with a liberal dose of Bible verses. Often this rambling type of prayer uses the word 'just' as frequently and as meaninglessly as many people use four-letter words in speech.

The effectiveness of a prayer does not depend on its length: we are not heard for our much speaking, as the Lord observed.

The follow-up to the service

We have already seen the need for follow-up and now we must look at the subject in detail. It is only too easy simply to assume that the minister will look after that!

Those who have been healed

These people will need encouragement and redirection in the light of their experience if the healing is to be maintained and deepened.

Note that Jesus nearly always told people to keep quiet about their healings. We should follow that practice and avoid getting the person to stand up and give a testimony, as is done in some services.

This is for several reasons:
- the system needs peace and quiet to adjust to the healing;
- the time will come when it is right to bear witness to what the Lord has done but, in the immediate aftermath of a healing, it is too easy to become emotionally unhealthy and hysterical about it;
- the people who have been healed may experience hostility if they speak about their experiences too soon when they return to family, friends and church. (I have had some unfortunate experiences of this.) Once they have grown stronger in faith, having found new friends to back them up, they will be able to cope.

Those who have not been healed

These people also need attention, and, oddly enough, many of those now in this ministry are those who were *not* healed – the present writer included! They need to be able to face the question which they are naturally asking – 'Why?'

There needs to be a fellowship of some sort in which both the above categories can be dealt with. It cannot be left to the minister. In the event of such a healing service producing results the minister will find that a lot of time is involved in this follow-up. Since most ministers are overstretched already, this will mean that many ministerial activities which are accepted as normal will have to be neglected. The congregation as a whole must be made to understand this, and readjust its expectations accordingly.

Counselling and follow-up

When people come for healing and seem to need counselling, it seems natural to hand them on to the minister.

This may not be wise for several reasons:

– Counselling involves regular appointments and the nature of a minister's work makes it difficult to undertake this responsibly.

– Even if the minister has had some training in counselling, this is often not at sufficient depth to qualify for in-depth probing and not all ministers are temperamentally suited to this work even if they are concerned with healing.

– The minister, unlike the counsellor, has little protection of privacy since the telephone number and the address of the manse are public knowledge. The minister is very much at the mercy of what Martin Israel describes as 'predatory love'.[1] Such people can destroy the family life at the manse, calling or phoning at all hours.

– A proper counsellor has a supervisor and, if the client starts forming a dependency, the supervisor can take action to save the counsellor, transferring the patient to another counsellor. The minister has no such protection, although ministers who are men may find that their wives spot dependencies! There is usually no church discipline by which the client can be transferred to another minister.

– If the patient is known personally to the minister there may be factors which inhibit discussion. For example, a lady came to the Christian Fellowship of Healing because she was a close friend of her minister. Her problem lay in that her father – an elder of that church – had abused her. She did not want to lay bare her soul to somebody she was going to meet socially, and she did not want to cause her father, whom she loved, and her minister a lot of trouble. There are many cases such as this in which a degree of anonymity is vital.

For these reasons, it is wise to know where appropriate counsel-

1 *The Spirit of Counsel*, Hodder, 1983.

ling is available so that the minister can exercise a prayerful ministry backing up the counselling.

On the other hand, if members of the team have been taught some 'Christian listening' techniques and have an openness to the people to whom they have ministered, they can take on most of the normal follow-up. This is where the New Testament principle of sending disciples out in pairs comes in. Such follow-up should be with a team of two people, preferably a man and a woman. Individuals who follow-up should be closely monitored lest they become unhealthily involved.

A welcoming family or 'spiritual scalp-hunting'?

Naturally, in and through all this, we hope that we will be able to welcome people into the Family of God. That is as it should be.

Yet there is a very fine distinction between two attitudes: using the healing service as a way of getting more recruits for our congregation or group – 'spiritual scalp-hunting'; and having a fellowship into which we can welcome people so that they can follow-up their healing – being a welcoming family.

On the surface these two look very similar but the difference is profound.

This leads us to consider the whole question of congregational life. The normal pattern of meetings in most congregations does not meet the need of somebody who has been awoken to the need for spiritual growth. There must be groups or courses which explore the Bible more deeply, which lead into a deeper prayer life and which explore the meaning of discipleship in the wider world today.

To use the Lord's Parable of the Sower (Mark 4.1): 'If the ground in which the new seed has been sown is thin and poor, however good the seed, it cannot take root.'

Too often we see the sad story of what happens in somebody in whom good seed has been sown. They show all the signs of having been 'born again' – a hunger for the Word of God, a need for deeper fellowship, and a reaching out to find a real mission in the world – only to be left to wither because the congregation offered no good soil. If you are praying for a spiritual harvest, first prepare the soil!

All of this takes us back to the rather surprisingly negative point with which we began: healing services are *not* a good idea unless they serve to give expression to an ongoing ministry of healing at the personal level day by day. They are not to be regarded as an extra activity to be laid on in the hope that people will become interested.

The order of service

A different order of service?

If you are starting afresh rather than building onto an existing service, then perhaps it might be wise to consider quite a different form of service. After all there are things to be done in a healing service which do not have the same emphasis in the ordinary worship of the Church, and there are things to be done in ordinary worship which we do not need to do in a healing service.

As an example of what should be included in a healing service but not in regular worship, we might look at the healing of relationships. We all know that resentment and lack of forgiveness can cause illness, and Jesus repeatedly tells us that it vitiates prayer.

Therefore it is wise to have some part of the service which relates in depth to our relationships, bringing them into the light of the Love of God before we come to physical healing. Obviously this will come into the normal parish worship from time to time, and there is an element of it each time we say the Lord's Prayer, but a healing service requires that we spend some time looking at this very sensitive area.

Praise and adoration

The Charismatic movement has always stressed the healing power of praise and adoration, and surely this is right. We praise God, not because God is not praise-seeking like an unhealthy child, but because if you love somebody you have to express that love, and it is unhealthy to 'keep it in'. Because God loves us He wants us to enjoy Him in the way described by the Shorter Catechism: 'Man's chief end is to glorify God and to enjoy Him forever.'

We express our love for God best in song, and we rightly enjoy doing so. Therefore there are no prayers of adoration and praise in the following sections. Praise and adoration are best left to the hymns and choruses.

Choruses

This leads us to one final note before we look at the order of service. Many ministers are prejudiced against choruses yet there are many which are Biblical and unsentimental. There are also Taizé chants which used thoughtfully can be of real value, while John Bell's *Come All You People*[1] offers shorter songs for worship. They break up the service into blocks, enabling us to express our response to what has been said, yet they do not require that we should stand up to sing a number of verses in the way a hymn does. This, as I have already mentioned, is important when there are people who are unwell in the congregation. I would therefore suggest that those who normally scorn them look again and perhaps find unexpected gold!

1 Wild Goose Publications, 1994, Glasgow

A possible order of service

Welcome: Since there are often strangers present, this needs to be more than a formality. People need to be put at their ease. For instance, if you talk to non-Church people, you will find that they are afraid of coming to church, not knowing when to stand, sit or kneel. These seem minor issues to church-folk, but if we have people who are new to the service it is wise to clear this up, and to make it plain that if people want to remain seated during a hymn, then they are welcome to do so. This is an important point to make clear, especially in a service in which there are people who are feeling unwell. If it is not obvious already it would be wise to indicate where the lavatories are, and to say that it is all right for people to head for them as necessary. In some churches it would be wise to add that the service will probably take about an hour, but that if there are a lot of people coming forward it might take longer. Therefore if people have buses to catch, taxis ordered etc. it is important to say, 'we quite understand if you leave before the end'.

Hymn: A well known, easily sung hymn, joyful and preferably with a chorus.

Prayer of approach: Introduced briefly, perhaps with a Bible verse.

Chorus: A chorus, sung seated following the line of the prayer.

Confession: Giving expression to the hurts and negative feelings in the congregation, giving vent to our need for cleansing, help and healing. (In some cases this might logically follow the Gospel.)

Hymn: Giving thanks for forgiveness.

Gospel: Read and explain a story of Jesus' healing.

Chorus

The healing of relationships: Introduced with words such as, 'Before we seek healing for our bodies, let us seek healing for relationships which have gone wrong, which are not as loving as they should be'.

Hymn or chorus

Invitation to receive healing or blessing: Explain simply the actual mechanics of what people should do. Give the congregation instructions on their part in prayer. Point people away from thinking of us as 'healers'. Assure them of the Lord's Presence.

Invocation: Thinking of the Lord's presence leads us into prayer invoking that Presence.

Healing: Perhaps choruses, Taizé chants etc. will be sung quietly, led by somebody prayerfully. Perhaps the Prayer of Intercession can be brought in at this point while individuals are receiving ministry. We should include at least some minutes of silence in which names can be mentioned out loud.

Thanksgiving and home-going prayer

Hymn of thanks and dedication

Benediction: As discussed earlier, this gives the whole congregation the laying-on of hands.

An omission?

I know that some of my colleagues will say that there is a serious omission in this order of service – there is no call to 'give your life to Jesus' before the healing.

This is no oversight. I do not see Jesus making it a condition of His healing that people should first become disciples. Some, such as Bartimaeus (Mark 10.52) and Mary of Magdala (Mark 16.9) did respond by 'following Him in the Way' (the early term used to describe becoming a Christian) but He did not make it a condition. In fact His healing was an aspect of the unconditional Love of God. Many of those whom He healed had not heard Him preach, e.g. the 'man born blind' (John 9.1), and the deaf-mute (Mark 7.31), so we cannot say that he healed only those who had repented as the result of His preaching.

It is totally out of character to suggest that Jesus will only heal you if you commit your life to Him. Of course, the other side of this is that true wholeness does involve loving God, loving neighbours and loving enemies as a response to the Gospel. Yet it is God who takes the initiative in healing.

We have, therefore, to preach the Good News and express it in healing. Then, if people respond, that is wonderful. Our final prayer and hymn should aim at leading people into a commitment, or into deeper commitment, and then the follow-up should consolidate the movement.

Introduction to the prayers

The prayers fall into four different sections. The first section consists of three possible alternatives for each prayer mentioned in the order of service; the second offers prayers based on the Celtic pattern; the third offers ideas for guided silence; and the fourth suggests a liturgical use for songs which are popular on the more charismatic side.

We have already noted one or two points about prayers. For example, if people are strange to the procedure or feeling unwell, it is not a good idea to have long prayers such as those which are common in many Church of Scotland services. As a matter of fact, this is more important than we might think – a retired minister I know did a sort of 'consumer check' on the services at his local church, and found that it was the long prayers which put people off more than anything else!

We also noted that while normal worship has to cover many aspects of the life of the Church and of the community, a healing service concentrates on one aspect. The prayers need to be less wide-ranging, but they do have to be more penetrating personally.

On the other hand, while there is a need for brevity there is also an important agenda in a healing service, and this must be covered. Cutting the prayers down too much can impoverish the service. Therefore the prayers offered here are for the most part broken up into short sections which are separated by a response which can be spoken or sung. They are also suitable for being shared out, with the prayers coming from the congregation rather than from the minister. Those taking part can be told to adapt their parts if they feel so inspired, provided that they do not make the prayer too long and that they finish with the words given, so that those leading the response and/or the next section know where they are.

Responses

I know that responses will be regarded with suspicion by many with a Church of Scotland background. However, this does not seem to apply when the response is sung to a tune which does not sound like a chant! There are plenty of such in *Songs for God's*

People[1] and in *The Iona Community Worship Book*.[2] Examples of responses are given later in this book as well.

Prayers

The prayer of approach would follow a brief welcome and an invitation, probably Biblical, to seek God's Presence together.

The prayer of confession takes up some of the themes in the approach, but leads into a more definite act of forgiveness. It too would probably be introduced by relevant Biblical verses. In some cases this prayer might be more appropriate *after* the 'looking at Jesus' section.

The prayer for the healing of relationships is new to most people who conduct worship, yet it is so vital before we seek physical healing. It is an important part of the Lord's Prayer – 'Forgive us as we have been forgiven' – and it should find a place in any healing service.

The prayer of intercession is in a form which tries to cope with a long list of people needing prayer. These lists of names and complaints can be very depressing! Hence I suggest ways in which we can keep referring the thoughts of the congregation back to Our Lord, tending to think about aspects of *His* Work, rather than naming diseases. Having done that we *express* healing love towards those named. This is more positive than prayers which plead with God tō listen to us. Actually it is we who ought to be listening to Him!

The prayer of invocation can be done in the privacy of the prayers before the service if one prefers to do it that way, as suggested earlier.

The prayers of healing and blessing are explained in a previous chapter.

1 Panel of Worship, The Church of Scotland, Oxford University Press, 1988
2 Wild Goose Publications, Glasgow, 1991

The prayers of thanksgiving and homegoing are designed to send us on our way.

These prayers are deliberately very diverse in style, for the main aim is not that people should adopt any one style or even that they should use these prayers as they stand. Rather, the aim is to stimulate thought and prayer so that truly relevant prayers may emerge to offer a link between God and His People. I find that most ministers use books of prayers as quarries out of which to dig ideas to inspire their own prayers, and I do not expect people to lift the prayers here and use them word for word.

In the prayers, words in capitals should be spoken as a response by all. Words in italics are instructions and should not be spoken.

Prayer of approach 1

One could treat the recurring phrase 'At Your invitation, LORD WE COME TO YOU' as versicle/response, or it could even be adapted to a simple tune.

Jesus said: 'Come to me all you who are weary and burdened and I will give you rest.' *(Matt. 11.28)*
Let us accept this, His invitation, as we turn to Him in prayer:

O Living God, Maker of all things,
we thank You that in Jesus we see
that You care for each of us individually,
and that You invite us to come to You for help and comfort.

You are the Holy One, greater than human minds can take in,
yet in Jesus we find that we can call You 'Abba, Father'.

In You we live and move and have our being,
yet in Jesus we face the fact that we can ignore You,
reject You, crucify You.

So now we accept Your gracious invitation,
and turn to You with our burdens and our weariness,
our hurts and our fears,
the wrong we have done and the wrong that we have suffered.

Father, welcoming Your children
who have wandered off the right path into darkness and danger.
At Your invitation, LORD WE COME TO YOU.

Lord Jesus,
You did not come to condemn us for where we went wrong,
but to save us from ourselves,
to heal our hurts and to reconcile us to God and to each other.
At Your invitation, LORD WE COME TO YOU.

Holy Spirit, Comforter
– yet also the fire which burns away our impurities
and the power with which to do the work
which Jesus has given us.
At Your invitation, LORD WE COME TO YOU.

In the light of the mystery of the Love of God,
Father, Son and Holy Spirit,
for ever One, and for ever Love, we bow.
May each of us know Your Word speaking in the silence.
Be still and know that I am God. *(silence)*

In Your Presence, we are truly at home at last,
in Your Presence, we can be our true selves at last,
in Your Presence, we can forget ourselves at last,
and find the true purpose of our lives
through Jesus Christ Our Lord, Amen.

Prayer of approach 2 (for Easter)

The response used here is drawn from Taizé.[1] It begins with three notes hummed, providing a lead-in.

Then came Jesus and stood in the midst and said, 'Peace be unto you. Then He showed them His Hands and His Side, saying, 'It is I myself, do not be afraid.' *(John 20.19)*

Let us adore Him who is our Risen Lord
and who comes to meet us now.

Lord Jesus, death and darkness could not hold You,
and even our rejection of You and our disbelief
cannot make You reject us.
WE ADORE YOU LORD JESUS CHRIST

By Your death and bitter Passion
You destroyed Satan's hold over us.
WE ADORE YOU LORD JESUS CHRIST

By Your wounds and by Your body broken,
our wounds and our brokenness are healed.
WE ADORE YOU LORD JESUS CHRIST

By Your Risen Presence we know that death has lost its sting
and the grave has lost its victory.
WE ADORE YOU LORD JESUS CHRIST

By Your gift of the Holy Spirit to us, your disciples today,
You enable us to continue Your Work.
WE ADORE YOU LORD JESUS CHRIST

1 'Adoramus te domine' is published in *Songs and Prayers from Taizé, Les Presses de Taizé, 71460 Taizé, France*

By Your Word of Peace, You give us Peace,
the Peace the world cannot give.
WE ADORE YOU LORD JESUS CHRIST

Forgiven, we forgive
– and forgiving others we are forgiven.
WE ADORE YOU LORD JESUS CHRIST

By Your victory
You make us more than conquerors in all things.
WE ADORE YOU LORD JESUS CHRIST

Lord of all life and power,
through the mighty resurrection of Your Son,
You overcame the old order of sin and death
to make all things new in Him;
grant that we, dying to sin,
and coming alive to Jesus Christ,
may rise to newness of life, here in this world,
and rise to share His Glory hereafter.
This we ask through Jesus Christ Our Risen Lord, Amen.

Prayer of approach 3

There is a 'Kyrie' (no. 61 in Songs for God's People[1]) but it is rather long. There are shorter ones in the Taizé collections, and in Come All You People, Sent by the Lord and Many and Great.[2]

'Jesus went round all their towns and villages, preaching the Gospel of the Kingdom and healing every sickness and disease. But when he saw the crowds, he was moved with compassion, they were like sheep without a shepherd, harassed and helpless.' *(Matt. 9.36)*

Jesus is the same, yesterday today and for ever.
Still He comes to us,
so let us be quietly and prayerfully aware of His Presence
as we pray:

Jesus, as you come to our town tonight,
still you look on the crowds in our streets with compassion,
sheep without a shepherd, at the mercy of false shepherds,
victims of all sorts of destructive forces.
Lord have mercy on us all. KYRIE ELEISON

Still the great harvest of human misery and suffering
waits for reapers.
Lord have mercy on us all. KYRIE ELEISON

Some of our troubles we have brought on ourselves
by our wrong living.
Some of our troubles come from the wrong living
of our families, of our communities.
Lord have mercy on us all. KYRIE ELEISON

1 Panel of Worship, The Church of Scotland, Oxford University Press, 1988
2 Wild Goose Publications, Glasgow

We need your light,
we need your forgiveness,
we need your healing,
we need you,
so we come to you.

*Chorus (Use a Common Metre tune such as 'Kilmarnock' which
can be found in most hymn books.)*
I come to You, Lord Jesus Christ,
bless me, Lord, even me.
Your Grace Your mercy and Your Peace,
cleanse, heal and set me free.

'The Son of Man is come to seek and to save that which was lost.'
And that means us, Lord.
THANK GOD YOU'VE COME

'I am come not to condemn but to save ... to rescue.'
And we certainly need to be rescued.
THANK GOD YOU'VE COME

'I am come that you may have life and have it in all its fullness.'
And we who are only half alive cry:
THANK GOD YOU'VE COME

The Kingdom of God is in our midst tonight,
Light and Life arise for our healing.
Now are we children of God
for at Your coming, Lord, death and darkness must flee.
and we can rise to find our true being
as Our Father's beloved children.

Glory be to The Father and to The Son and to the Holy Spirit,
As it was in the beginning is now and ever shall be,
world without end, Amen.

Chorus (Again to the tune 'Kilmarnock')
Thank God You've come O Gracious Lord,
Thank God You've come to me,
Thank God You've come not to condemn,
But now to set me free.

Prayer of confession 1

When leading this prayer, we should make it obvious by our actions that we are reading the promises from the Bible. Possibly have a reader for the Bible verse and a pray-er who responds.

Hear the Good News – The Gospel of God's forgiving Love:
'There is joy in the presence of the angels of God over one sinner who repents.' *(Luke 15.10)*
Let us therefore bring joy to the courts of Heaven!
Lord have mercy. CHRIST HAVE MERCY.

'Here is a trustworthy saying that deserves full acceptance: Christ Jesus came into the world to save sinners, of whom I am the worst, but for that very reason mercy was shown to me, so that in me Christ Jesus might display His unlimited patience.' *(1 Tim. 1.15)*
Let us take that assurance to ourselves,
and cast ourselves on His unlimited patience.
Lord have mercy. CHRIST HAVE MERCY.

'God is Light, and in Him there is no darkness at all. If we walk in the light as He is in the Light, we have fellowship with each other and the Blood of Jesus His Son cleanses us from all sin.' *(1 John 1.5-7)*
Let us walk into His glorious Light,
knowing that our sins are forgiven,
and cleansed by the Blood of Christ
– His Agony over us all upon the Cross.
Lord have mercy. CHRIST HAVE MERCY.

'If we say we have no sin, we deceive ourselves and the truth is not in us, but if we confess our sins, He is faithful and just to forgive us our sins and to cleanse us from all unrighteousness.' *(1 John 1.9)*
Let us therefore put aside all excuses, drop all shams,
stop blaming others and face the truth before Him,
assured that in the light of His forgiveness,

all the half-truths with which we protect ourselves,
are no longer needed.
In silence let us face the truth before Him.
(silence)
Lord have mercy. CHRIST HAVE MERCY.

'Surely He has borne our griefs and carried our sorrows ... and the
Lord laid on Him the iniquity of us all.' *(Is. 53.4)*
Know therefore, that in His Love for you,
He has taken Your sins and your hurts on Himself.
Your sins are no longer yours, but His.
Your griefs and sorrows are His.
Your hurts and wounds are His too. ALLELUIA

O Loving God, it seems so unfair
that You should take our sins on Yourself like that,
yet the justice of Your Love is true justice,
and in Love You take our load so that we may be free.
Gratefully we accept Your offer,
and avail ourselves of the power
to make a new beginning, cleansed and renewed. ALLELUIA

Now, as new men and new women we face the future,
knowing that the past is dealt with.
We go forward forgiving
as we have been forgiven through Jesus Christ Our Lord. ALLELUIA
Amen.

Prayer of confession 2

This prayer is especially suitable for dividing into sections, each given to a different person in the congregation, so that the prayer comes from the body of the congregation, the minister opening and closing it. A selection of verses from Isaiah chapter 1 could introduce this prayer. A 'Kyrie' could be used instead of 'Christ have mercy'.

(Minister)
O God, Our Father, we, Your children, cry to You.
You gave us the gift of life
and set us in this world to fulfil Your purposes
but we have misused the gift of life,
destroying ourselves and the world around us.
We have crucified Your Love,
the very Love upon which we depend for life.

Sick and ashamed we come before You
seeking forgiveness and healing,
both for ourselves and for our world.

(The following sections could come from the body of the congregation.)

(Reader 1)
Some of us cry to You because we are racked with pain,
weakness overtakes us,
and human resources have come to an end.
Lord have mercy. CHRIST HAVE MERCY.

(Reader 2)
Some of us have blundered into darkness,
we have lost the way,
and are now plagued by fear, despair and depression.
Lord have mercy. CHRIST HAVE MERCY.

(Reader 3)
Some of us come from homes
where there is strife, bitterness and quarrels,
homes in which love has been poisoned by human sin.
Lord have mercy. CHRIST HAVE MERCY.

(Reader 4)
Some of us come agonizing over a loved one
who has gone wrong,
and we come bearing the burden of another's sin and shame.
Lord have mercy. CHRIST HAVE MERCY.

(Reader 5)
Some of us are nearing the end of our earthly journey,
and we need to know that You are with us
as we draw near the Valley of the Shadow.
Lord have mercy. CHRIST HAVE MERCY.

(Minister)
Some of us are Your disciples,
gathered here to meet the great needs
of those who come to seek You.
We have failed to heal and help so often,
and the burden of human suffering and our own inadequacy
lies heavy upon us.
We have nothing to offer those who come
unless You pour out Your Spirit upon us afresh.

Lord, You know our weakness, You know that we love You.
Lord have mercy. CHRIST HAVE MERCY.

'The Lord is gracious and full of compassion, near to all who call
upon Him in sincerity.' *(Ps. 145.8 and 145.18)*
Gracious and merciful Lord,
Your forgiveness flows from the Cross to cover all our sin.
Your Hand is outstretched to heal and bless each one of us.
Your Spirit is poured out plentifully upon us,
and so we go forward rejoicing.

Surely You are in the midst of us Lord,
and the Light of Your Face shines upon us,
through Jesus Christ Our Lord, Amen.

Prayer of confession 3

'God so loved the world that He gave His only begotten Son that whoever believes in Him shall not perish but have eternal life. God sent not His Son into the world to condemn the world but that the world through Him might be saved.' *(John 3.16)*

Since God loves the world, including You and me, in this way, let us take stock afresh of our lives. Let us pray:

O God, Our Father,
we look once more at the costly love,
which agonizes over each of us,
and we know that we have become separated from You
by our sin and by our folly.
To You we cry: KYRIE ELEISON

We too have chosen the darkness of selfish living
rather than the light of Your Love,
and we are part of the world's problems,
which result from our wrong choices.
Before we destroy ourselves and our world,
To You we cry: KYRIE ELEISON

Still You come, as You came long ago,
not to condemn us for where we have gone wrong,
but to save us,
taking on Yourself our sicknesses, sorrows and sins,
making them Your own,
so that we may be free to begin afresh.
To You we cry: KYRIE ELEISON

We know that no superficial healing,
no new set of good resolutions,
no good advice can meet our need.
We need to be re-made, born again,
raised up out of our deadness,
and only Your Power can do that, so,
To You we cry: KYRIE ELEISON

Our sick and broken humanity
we bring to the foot of Your Cross.
In silence we remember our own faults and failings.
(Silence)
In the Light of Your promised forgiveness,
To You we cry: KYRIE ELEISON

Over each who truly turns to You,
may Your mercy flow now.
May each who begins to realize Your Love,
know Your words spoken over them:
'Father forgive them, they know not what they do.'
(Silence)

Praise be to God, who comes to meet us now, in this place,
to give us new light, new life, new love.
By the renewing Power of the Holy Spirit upon us,
may we begin afresh today/tonight,
however far we may have wandered from the way,
however deeply we have been hurt.

Now to Him who is able to do far more
than we ever ask or imagine,
according to the power which is at work within us,
to Him be glory and praise for ever, Amen.

The healing of relationships 1

'Make every effort to keep the unity of the Spirit in the bond of peace ... be kind and compassionate to each other, forgiving even as in Christ God forgave you.' *(Ephesians 4.3)*
Let us now make that effort to deepen our unity
and to strengthen the bond of peace.

Let us express our readiness to forgive others in prayer here,
that we may follow it up, when the time is right,
and find reconciliation, if there is readiness on the other side.
Let us therefore prepare ourselves to say the Lord's Prayer
and mean it.

O God, Our Father,
we, Your quarrelsome family come before You.
May Your Holy Spirit guide us now
to see if there is any wrong relationship
interfering with the healing work of Your Church.
So may we be able to pray truly in the Power of the Spirit
and in the Peace of Christ.

We remember before You
those who, unknown to us, feel that we have wronged them.

We remember before You
those whom we know that we have wronged
and whom we find it hard to face.

We remember before You
those whose way of life, or whose way of speaking annoys us,
and whom we reject.

We remember before You
the sins and hurts passed down in our families
from generation to generation.

We remember before You
the sins of Your Church,
and our part in all the bigotry and the prejudice,
the hypocrisy and the infighting
which disrupt our unity and bring disgrace
on the very name of 'Christian'.

We seek afresh Your forgiveness
for our part in all these wrong relationships,
especially for the times when we were sure we were in the right,
but hurt others by our arrogance.

As for our fellow sinners whose sins have hurt us,
we forgive them, and pray that somehow, sometime,
we may find the way to put things right.

If they are unwilling to be reconciled,
we hand over judgement to You,
for You alone know the secrets of all hearts.

If they are beyond our reach, in this world or beyond death,
then we surrender into Your Hands these relationships.
Your Peace be between us and them.

Now, as fellow sinners and as fellow sufferers,
looking to the one God and Father of us all, we pray:
OUR FATHER ...

Now let us strengthen the bond of unity
as we share the Peace of the Lord Jesus with each other.
(Pass around The Peace.)

The healing of relationships 2

'God was reconciling the world to Himself in Christ, not counting people's sins against them, and has passed on to us the ministry of reconciliation.' *(II Cor. 5.19)*

Let us pray:
Lord Jesus, reconciling us to each other and to God,
pour out Your Spirit upon us,
that there may be a real work of reconciliation in our midst now.

We remember the parents who brought us into the world –
those still with us, and those who have died before us.
We give thanks for any way
in which they mirrored Your Love to us,
May Your Mercy to cover any harm or hurt they did us,
or we did them.
Lord have mercy. CHRIST HAVE MERCY.

We remember neighbours –
past and present, good neighbours and bad neighbours.
We remember friends –
good friends and those who let us down.
We remember those beside whom we worked –
those who were good to be with
and those who were a problem to us.
We give thanks for every good relationship,
and seek Your Mercy for relationships which went wrong,
whoever was at fault.
May Your Mercy to cover any harm or hurt
which these whom we have remembered did us, or we did them.
Lord have mercy. CHRIST HAVE MERCY.

We remember those whose work was meant to help us –
doctors, teachers, dentists, nurses, officials
and all the ordinary folk in shops and offices.
We give thanks for all skill and care which has helped us.
May Your Mercy to cover any harm or hurt they did us,
or we did them.
Lord have mercy. CHRIST HAVE MERCY.

We remember those who needed us to help them,
who needed our skill, our care, our prayers.
We give thanks for any way
in which we were able to mirror Your Love to them.
We ask for Your Mercy to cover any harm we did,
or any good we failed to do in their time of need.
Lord have mercy. CHRIST HAVE MERCY.

We remember those whose suffering cries out for healing,
disturbing our peace;
those whose plight cries out for justice,
and whose misery challenges our right to be comfortable.
We give thanks for any way in which we can respond to their need.
Have mercy on our weakness,
on our slowness to respond to Your Spirit.
Lord have mercy. CHRIST HAVE MERCY.

Now, with this work of reconciliation done,
we would pray as one family,
as fellow sufferers and fellow sinners:
OUR FATHER ...

Let us now share the Peace with each other. *(Pass around the Peace.)*

The healing of Relationships 3

Jesus tells us that we must forgive as we have been forgiven – indeed it is only those who have been forgiven much who can truly forgive much, and in so doing they are themselves forgiven.

Let us ensure that this healing, creative cycle of forgiving and being forgiven goes on flowing here tonight/today.

In quietness now let us name before God
the people in our families who have hurt us
and have caused trouble. *(Silence)*
And those who think that we have caused trouble. *(silence)*
We remember not only those who are living
but those who have died. *(silence)*
We remember especially those who have died
leaving poison behind in the family. *(silence)*
As part of the family, sharing its guilt and shame, we pray:
Lord have mercy on them and forgive us as we forgive them.

The friends we have met on life's journey have not been perfect,
neither are we.
Let us remember before God
those relationships that have led to ill-feeling. *(silence)*
Let us surrender to God the right to judge
who was to blame. *(silence)*
Only You, Lord, know the true rights and wrongs of the situation.
Lord have mercy upon them and forgive us as we forgive them.

We think of people we like, and those whom we find hard to like.
 And those who find it hard to like us.
Those we understand, and those whom we find hard to understand.
And those who find it hard to understand us.
Only Your Love can lift us above our likes and dislikes

into that love which is our peace.
Lord have mercy on them and forgive us as we forgive them.

The world is full of strife and war, famine and violence,
and we are part of that world.
Let us remember before God those who are troublemakers,
those who seem to be a threat to our peace. *(silence)*
Let us remember that they probably see us as troublemakers
and a threat to their peace. *(silence)*
Lord have mercy upon them, and forgive us as we forgive them.

Father, we Your quarrelsome children,
pray for this world which You have entrusted to us.
Grant us grace to work for peace without taking the easy way out;
to work for justice without causing more trouble;
to work for Your Kingdom without being fanatical.
So may Your Name be hallowed and respected.
May Your Kingdom be established in our world
as we learn to do Your Will.
May injustice, poverty and famine be abolished
as we all share our daily bread.
By the flow of Your forgiveness through us,
may the relationships between individuals and nations
be cleansed and healed.

And as we face all the dangers and problems ahead,
knowing our weaknesses as fellow human beings,
we pray for Your Salvation to deliver us
from the evil into which we fall so easily
– as individuals, as churches, as part of humanity.
Therefore together we pray:
OUR FATHER ...
Let us now share the Peace with each other. *(Pass around the peace.)*

Prayer of intercession 1

This prayer is based upon St John's Gospel.

Lord Jesus,
You told us that if we abide in You, with Your Word in us,
then we can ask in Your Name and it shall be done.
May Your Word so live in us,
that loving one another, and abiding in You,
our prayers may be a lifeline of healing for these in need.

Lord, You are peace, and You give us Your peace,
May Your peace now enfold:
(Here include the names of those in distress, depression etc.)

Thanks be to God for the Peace of the Lord Jesus
now enfolding these His beloved children.
Praise ye the Lord. THE LORD'S NAME BE PRAISED.

Lord You are light, the light that heals and is life-giving,
May Your light now shine on:
(Here include the names of those with medical and surgical troubles.)

Thanks be to God for the healing light of Christ
shining now upon these His beloved children.
Praise ye the Lord: THE LORD'S NAME BE PRAISED.

Lord You are love, the love that casts out all fear,
May Your love now set free from the bondage of fear:
(Here include the names of those with phobias, worries, etc.)

Thanks be to God for His love, now overcoming fear,
for these His beloved children.
Praise ye the Lord. THE LORD'S NAME BE PRAISED.

Lord You are Resurrection and Life,
conquering death and filling us with new life. Fill with new life:
(Here include the names of those with so-called terminal illnesses.)

Thanks be to God that His Spirit
which raised Christ from the dead
is now raising up these His beloved children.
Praise ye the Lord. THE LORD'S NAME BE PRAISED.

Lord You are the Good Shepherd,
carrying the lambs in Your arms.
We lift these children, and these expectant mothers, up to You.
(Here include the names of children and/or pregnant mothers.)

Thanks be to God for the Good Shepherd's love
now blessing these His little ones.
Praise ye the Lord. THE LORD'S NAME BE PRAISED.

(Add extra categories as needed using the same basic pattern)

Lord, You are the True Vine and we are Your branches,
linked together, sharing the common life in Christ,
so now we share our concern for one another,
remembering before You the needs of:
(Here include the names of fellow-members in need.)

Thanks be to God for the life-giving flow of His Love
blessing these with whom we are united in Christ.
Praise ye the Lord. THE LORD'S NAME BE PRAISED.

Glory be to the Father who loves us,
Glory be to Jesus, the Word of God made flesh for us,
Glory be to the Holy Spirit filling our lives with love and power,
Glory be to God, the One God who is eternally Love.
Alleluia. Amen.

Prayer of intercession 2

This prayer is based on the Synoptic Gospels, and the response is adapted from Psalm 129.8

'They brought to Jesus all who were diseased and those who had a demon, and He healed many and cast out many demons.' *(Mark 1.32)*

So let us bring to Him the names of those who are suffering,
knowing that even if they are only names to us,
each is known to Him.
Let us pray:

Lord Jesus, you opened the eyes of the blind,
the ears of the deaf and the mouths of the dumb,
so we bring to You:
(Here include the names of the deaf, the blind and of those with speech problems.)

In the Name of Jesus we reach out to these in blessing:
The blessing of the Lord be upon you,
WE BLESS YOU IN THE NAME OF THE LORD JESUS.

Lord Jesus, You raised up the paralysed,
restored withered limbs and set invalids on their feet,
so we bring to You:
(Here include the names of the medical and surgical cases.)

In the Name of Jesus we reach out to these in blessing:
The blessing of the Lord be upon you,
WE BLESS YOU IN THE NAME OF THE LORD JESUS.

Lord Jesus, You sought the lost,
You were the 'Friend of sinners',
and You brought forgiveness to the penitent,
so we bring to You:
(Here include the names of those who are 'going wrong'.)

In the Name of Jesus we reach out to these in blessing:
The blessing of the Lord be upon you,
WE BLESS YOU IN THE NAME OF THE LORD JESUS.

Lord Jesus, You raised up the dead,
cured the incurable, and You conquered death itself,
so we bring to You:
(Here include the so-called incurable and terminal cases.)

In the Name of Jesus we reach out to these in blessing:
The blessing of the Lord be upon you,
WE BLESS YOU IN THE NAME OF THE LORD JESUS.

Lord Jesus, You experienced darkness of soul in Gethesemane,
forsakenness on the Cross and You went down into death itself,
so we bring to You:
(Here include the names of those in depression.)

In the Name of Jesus we reach out to these in blessing:
The blessing of the Lord be upon you,
WE BLESS YOU IN THE NAME OF THE LORD JESUS.

Lord Jesus, You took babes in Your arms,
You were 'the Friend of children'
and you restored to their parents those who were ill,
so we bring to You:
(Here include the names of children.)

In the Name of Jesus we reach out to these in blessing:
The blessing of the Lord be upon you,
WE BLESS YOU IN THE NAME OF THE LORD JESUS.

Lord Jesus, You were born of woman,
entering this world as we do,
and as the Good Shepherd,
You 'gently lead those who are with young',
so we bring to You:
(Here include the names of pregnant mothers.)

In the Name of Jesus we reach out to these in blessing:
The blessing of the Lord be upon you,
WE BLESS YOU IN THE NAME OF THE LORD JESUS.

Lord Jesus, You have called us Your disciples,
uniting us in the Holy Spirit,
sharing each other's joys and sorrows,
so we bring to you our fellow members in need.
(Here include the names of those in the congregation, group or fellowship.)

In the Name of Jesus we reach out to these in blessing:
The blessing of the Lord be upon you,
WE BLESS YOU IN THE NAME OF THE LORD JESUS.

We pray for one another here, for each other's needs,
for our growing together in the Love and Power of Christ.
Unite us in Your Love, equip us with Your Power,
and bless us in Your Service.
This we ask for Your Own Name's sake, Amen.

Prayer of intercession 3

The previous prayers of intercession both carefully avoided mentioning specific illnesses, concentrating on the positive nature of Christ rather than on the negative nature of disease. In this prayer, however, we do name categories of illness. There are three ways in which to handle this prayer:

- *Leave a set time of silence for each category. Tell people how long it will be, e.g. 1 minute.*
- *Invite people to name anybody they know who falls into any category but not going into medical details.*
- *Sing a 'Kyrie' or some other chant or chorus after naming each category.*

The introductory and concluding prayers are based on Titus 2.11 and 3.4-6 (NEB[1]).

O God, Our Father,
we bless You that Your grace has dawned upon the world
with healing for all mankind,
and that You have richly poured out Your Spirit upon us,
so that we can pray as Your Family,
knowing that our prayers will be heard and answered
through Jesus Christ Our Lord.

We remember before You those having operations,
and those recovering. *(pause)*

We remember those with wasting diseases. *(pause)*

We remember those with depression and those with phobias. *(pause)*

We remember those with mental illnesses. *(pause)*

1 New English Bible, © Oxford University Press and Cambridge University Press, 1961, 1970.

We remember those with cancer. *(pause)*

We remember those suffering
from the multiple problems of old age. *(pause)*

(Any further categories can be included as necessary.)

We remember surgeons, doctors, nurses, hospital staff
and all who work for the good of those whom we have named.
We remember those in our parish and those in our congregation
who work with the sick-suffering.
May Your Wisdom guide them, blessing their human skills.
May Your Love sustain them when they are under pressure.
May your healing flow through them.

We remember those organizations which support research,
and which try to help people with specific diseases and problems:
Cancer Research, The Samaritans,
The Association for Research into Multiple Schlerosis,
(and any others which are especially relevant)
to those for whom we have prayed.
May Your Light guide them and bless their work.

We remember those who tend loved ones who are ill.
Sustain them with Your Patience,
and when human love has grown weary with costly caring,
may Your Spirit renew and refresh them.

And may the kindness and generosity of God Our Saviour
dawn on us all, more and more, until all the shadows are dispersed,
all sins left behind, all diseases healed, all suffering conquered,
and all relationships filled with the glory of His Love,
through Jesus Christ Our Lord, Amen.

Prayer of invocation 1

Jesus said, 'As the Father sent me, so I send you. Receive the Holy Spirit.' *(John 20.22)*

In Your Name, O Lord,
we face the suffering of Your children here today/tonight.

By Your Spirit within us,
the works that You did in Galilee long ago,
we shall also do here tonight:

By Your Authority we shall drive away all darkness;

By Your Power we shall heal the sick;

By Your Love we shall draw the lost home to the Father's love.

Glorify Your Name in us and through us,
that this building may echo
to the songs of praise and of thanksgiving.

Glory be to the Father and to the Son and to the Holy Spirit,
as it was in the beginning, is now and ever shall be,
world without end, Amen.

Prayer of invocation 2

This prayer can be divided into sections, each given to a different person in the congregation, so that the prayer comes from the body of the congregation, the minister opening and closing it.

(Minister)
O God Our Father, we rejoice that even now
You are gathering us to Yourself as a family,
drawing us to Yourself through Jesus.

(The following sections could come from the body of the congregation)

(Reader 1)
In love for You, and in compassion for our fellow human beings,
we open our hearts to You.
May Your Holy Spirit fill us, giving us love and power.
So may we bring Your healing to bear on those who seek you.

(Reader 2)
O Christ, You healed diseases, restored sight and hearing,
and You raised up the paralysed.
You are the same, yesterday, today and for ever.
Work through us now by the Power of Your Holy Spirit.

(Reader 3)
O Christ, You cast out demons, banished darkness,
and rescued the lost.
You are the same, yesterday, today and for ever.
Work through us now by the Power of Your Holy Spirit.

(Reader 4)

O Christ, You raised the dead, You went down into death itself,
and You conquered death for us.
You are the same, yesterday, today and for ever.
Work through us now by the Power of Your Holy Spirit.

(Reader 5)

O Christ, You called ordinary people to be Your disciples.
You sent them out to spread the Gospel
and to heal the sick, pouring out Your Spirit upon them.
You are the same, yesterday, today and for ever.
Work through us now by the Power of Your Holy Spirit.

(Minister)

May the Father's Love draw us to Himself,
may the Saviour's Love save the sick and the sinful,
may the Holy Spirit fill us all, so that our words and our actions
may be alive with the Glory of God.

Glory be to the Father and to the Son and to the Holy Spirit,
as it was in the beginning is now and ever shall be,
world without end, Amen.

Prayer of invocation 3

Jesus said, 'Will Your Heavenly Father not give the Holy Spirit to those who ask Him?' *(Luke 11.13)*
So let us confidently ask for the Holy Spirit to be poured out upon us.

Let us pray:
Heavenly Father, trusting in The Word of Your Son, Our Lord,
we ask for the inspiration of Your Holy Spirit now.

May Your Holy Spirit descend upon us afresh,
even as it did upon Jesus at His Baptism,
renewing in us the assurance that we are Your beloved children
in whom You delight.
Enable us to share this awareness
with those who are lost and unsure of their identity.

Holy Spirit, come upon us like a mighty rushing wind,
carrying off all the rubbish in our lives,
driving us forward in power,
breaking down all that holds Your children in bondage,
opening new doors, breathing new life into us.

Holy Spirit, come upon us as fire,
purifying us and setting us ablaze with love for God
and for our fellow sufferers,
until disease and darkness are burned up before us,
and the glory of the Lord is seen over us.

Holy Spirit, source of all true healing,
equip us with those gifts of the Spirit which we need
in order to be able to do the work of God this night/day.

Give us eyes that see through the pretences and the half-truths
in order that we may see the real needs
of those who come to seek healing.

Give us ears to hear the cry which people dare not utter.

Give us words which are Your Words,
a piercing two-edged sword,
strong to destroy the works of darkness.

Give us hands strong to do Your Work,
to reach out in Your Name to serve and to welcome,
to heal and to bless.

Since we are all gathered together of one accord,
may we be empowered to bear witness
to the Gospel of Your Kingdom with signs and wonders.

May we as individuals be unnoticed,
and may people go from here
knowing only that they have met with the Living God,
the Father, the Son and the Holy Spirit
to whom be glory and praise for ever, Amen.

Thanksgiving and homegoing 1

In this prayer we use the 'round' 'Rejoice in the Lord always'[1] using the whole round to begin and end the prayer, but using the twofold 'Rejoice' after the various phrases.

REJOICE IN THE LORD ALWAYS, AND AGAIN I SAY, REJOICE!

Let us pray.
We do indeed rejoice in You, O Lord,
and we rejoice in all that You have done for us this day/night.

In Our Father's House we have known Our Father's welcome.
REJOICE! REJOICE!

By Your Word You have cleansed us from old sins and wrongs.
REJOICE! REJOICE!

By Your broken Body You have healed our brokenness.
REJOICE! REJOICE!

By Your reconciling death you have healed our relationships.
REJOICE! REJOICE!

By the touch of Your Hand and the anointing of Your Grace
You have healed our sicknesses.
REJOICE! REJOICE!

By the Power of Your Spirit
You have enabled us to share in Your Work.
REJOICE! REJOICE!

1   Rejoice in the Lord Always, Evelyn Tarner, copyright © 1967 Sacred Songs/Word Music (UK), Administered by Copycare, PO Box 77, Hailsham, BN27 3EF, UK. Used by permission.

As we go from here into all that lies ahead of us,
enable us so to live,
that something of the Life of Jesus may be seen in us.
May we draw others into the experience
of the healing Love of God.
May we do such beautiful things
that people may glorify Our Father in Heaven.

Father, into Your Hands, we commit our lives,
and the lives of all our loved ones.
(silence)
Through Jesus Christ Our Lord, Amen.

REJOICE IN THE LORD ALWAYS, AND AGAIN I SAY, REJOICE!

Thanksgiving and homegoing 2

This prayer was written by Angela Crawford, who was a member of the Christian Fellowship of Healing, and it has·often been used by various people to conclude the monthly Healing Service.[1]

All glory and honour to You, Lord,
for all that has happened in this place tonight.

And may the Presence of Him who is with us now,
go with us as we return to our homes
and throughout the week ahead.

May the Light from the Face of Jesus so illumine our way
that we may see the world differently:
through His eyes.

May His Peace so enfold us and fill us
that we may carry it around us like a cloak,
secure and safe in Him.

May the Joy of knowing that we are children of the Risen Lord
fill us with that deep happiness
which the world can neither give nor take away.

Father, into Your Hands we commit our loved ones
wherever they may be. *(silence)*
Father into Your Hands we commit our lives,
through Jesus Christ Our Lord, Amen.

1 Used here with permission.

Thanksgiving and homegoing 3

O Father we thank You that this day/night
Your love has touched our lives.

For Your Word of pardon and of cleansing,
we give thanks and praise.

For Your Peace healing our relationships,
bringing reconciliation and understanding,
we give thanks and praise.

For Your Holy Spirit searching our hearts,
and healing old, forgotten hurts,
we give thanks and praise.

For Your Hand upon those who came sick in body,
we give thanks and praise.

In gratitude we offer these our lives to You afresh.
In the light of the Love we have glimpsed here,
may selfish living be left behind,
and a new life of love and power be opened up.

In the light of the needs of suffering people around us day by day,
we pray that we may grow in effectiveness
as we obey Your command to preach the Gospel
and to heal the sick

In the light of Your Cross and Resurrection,
make us more than conquerors in all our sufferings,
and make us alive with hope as we come to face death.

We pray for one another here:

May those who have received healing, receive grace to live it out,
to develop it and to glorify Your Name.

May those whose complete healing has not yet come,
be sustained with patience and with hope.

May those who do not seem to have received healing,
yet know that Your Grace is sufficient for them,
and experience Your Strength in their weakness.

Father, into Your hands we commit our lives,
and the lives of all our loved ones. *(silence)*

(Read these lines if it is an morning service.)
In Your Hands our future is safe, and life takes on new meaning.
So we travel on into the future with confidence,
for nothing can separate us from Your Love,
through Jesus Christ Our Lord, Amen.

(Read these lines if it is an evening service.)
Abide with us Lord, for it is towards evening and the day is far spent.
Abide with us, so that we, knowing Your Presence,
may sleep this night in that peace
which the world can neither give nor take away.

(Read these lines at both morning and evening services.)
Now to Him who is able to do far more
than we ever ask or imagine,
according to the power that is at work within us,
to Him be glory and praise in the Church,
through Jesus Christ Our Lord, Amen.

Prayers based on the celtic pattern

Introduction

This is another complete set of prayers with a distinctive approach. The recent resurgence of interest in the Celtic prayers gathered in the *Carmina Gadelica*[1] has had a profound influence on many of us. The prayers in this set owe a lot to this tradition, while not trying to imitate it.

There are four key characteristics of the old Celtic prayers:

- they are strongly Trinitarian;
- they have plentiful allusions to Bible stories;
- they are very aware of 'the great cloud of witnesses unseen' (Hebr. 12.1);
- they are well earthed in the realities of life, and in nature.

I hope that all the prayers in this book show these characteristics, but perhaps this set weaves in these themes more tightly.

---

1 Recently republished by Floris Books, Edinburgh, 1992.

Celtic style

Prayer of approach

In the Name of the Glorious Father,
we His children gather in this place.
the Blessing of Our Father in Heaven be upon us.

In the Name of Jesus Our Saviour, Our Healer and Our Lord,
we whom He has called gather in this place.
the Blessing of Jesus be upon us.

In the Name of the Holy Spirit of the sevenfold Gifts,
we, in the unity of Christ, gather in this place.
the blessing of the Holy Spirit the Strengthener be upon us.

May we be upheld by the prayer of the whole Church on earth,
may we be upheld by the prayers of the faithful departed,
may we be upheld by the angelic host.

In the Name of Jesus we would arm ourselves
that we may be strong in the Lord of Hosts
and in His Mighty Power.

The strong belt of the Gospel Truth gird us round,
the shining breastplate of Christ's Rightness cover our hearts,
the helmet of gracious Salvation be on our heads.

Our feet be shod with the Gospel of Peace to carry us forward,
the great shield of our Faith defend us and our loved ones,
the Sword of the Spirit, the Word of God,
destroy the works of darkness.

Now we arise to do the work of God.
to Our Glorious Father be glory,
to Jesus the True Healer be glory,
to the Holy Spirit, the Fire to set us aflame,
and the Wind to fill us with power, be glory,
to the Three who are one in Love be glory
this day and for ever, Amen.

Celtic style

Prayer of confession

O Christ of the endless mercies
we cry to You,
O Christ, unfailing fountain of goodness,
we cry to You,
O Christ the Saviour of the lost,
we cry to You.

Lost on the dark moor
because we ignored Your Word with its warnings.
Have mercy on us,
restore us to the right path for Your Name's sake.

Unclean because we sought pleasure and power in the wrong ways,
have mercy on us,
fill us with Your Joy as we walk Your Way.

Overwhelmed by the storms of life, and near to shipwreck,
have mercy on us,
come to us walking upon the very waves which make us fear,
and give us Your Peace.

Swiftly comes the Word of Your Peace to all who cry in sincerity,
surely comes Your Salvation to all who reach out in penitence,
certain are Your Promises of Forgiveness and New Life
to all who know their need.

'I came to seek and to save those who are lost',
Glory be to the Christ who has found us.

'Now You are clean by the Word which I speak to you'.
Glory be to the Christ who washes us clean.

'O you of little faith, why did you doubt? Peace to you.'
Glory be to the Christ who stills the storm and gives us peace.

Glory be to the Father of All Mercies,
Glory be to Jesus, Friend of Sinners,
Glory be to the Holy Spirit making us new,
to the One God be glory in the Church now and for ever, Amen.

Celtic style

Prayer for the healing of relationships

The Love of the God and Father of us all
 be upon us all, and let none be excluded.

The Cross of Christ be between us
and all whom we have met on life's journey.

The Spirit of Christ
complete the interweaving pattern of our relationships
until we raise up a High Cross to the glory of God.

Between us and those whom we loved,
but who turned and hurt us,
be the Peace of Christ.

Between us and those who seem to be our enemies,
be the Peace of Christ.

Between us and those whom we have wronged,
be the Peace of Christ.

Between us and those with whom we seek reconciliation,
be the Peace of Christ.

Between us and those with whom no reconciliation is possible,
be the Peace of Christ.

Between us and those who have passed beyond death,
be the Peace of Christ.

Between us and the earth which the Lord has entrusted to us,
be the Peace of Christ

Between us and the creatures with which we share the earth,
be the Peace of Christ

Between us and all the work which we do on earth,
be the Peace of Christ.

O Christ, the only true Judge,
into Your hands we surrender the rights and wrongs of the past,
neither condemning others, nor excusing them,
neither condemning ourselves, nor excusing ourselves.

The sins which led us to hurt each other and to misuse Your Earth,
we lay at the foot of Your Cross,
and with all our fellow sinners we look to You for Mercy,

By Your Life-Blood poured out upon the Cross,
take away all our sins,
those we committed and those committed against us,
and raise us all up to the New Life of Love in Your Kingdom.

Glory be to the Father who welcomes the prodigals,
Glory be to Jesus who makes Peace by His Cross,
Glory be to the Spirit of Love and Truth,
to the One God be glory for ever, Amen.

Celtic style

Prayer of intercession

Into the Love of the Father, we lift up His suffering children,
In the Name of Jesus, we face all that is dark and unhealthy,
In the Power of the Holy Spirit, we pray:

Peace, deep peace, be to those who suffer in their bodies,
(name them)
Peace be to each one,
The deep Peace of Christ the Son of Peace be to you.

Peace, deep peace, be to those who are oppressed by darkness,
(name them)
Peace be to each one,
The deep Peace of Christ the Son of Peace be to you.

Peace, deep peace, be to those who are mentally ill,
(name them)
Peace be to each one,
The deep Peace of Christ the Son of Peace be to you.

Peace, deep peace, be to those who grow old,
knowing confusion and pain,
(name them)
Peace be to each one,
The deep Peace of Christ the Son of Peace be to you.

(add extra categories as needed using the same basic pattern)

May the Wisdom of God
guide all medical staff who tend them.
May the Holiness of God
sanctify all earthly remedies and treatments.
May the Patience of God
uphold all family and friends who care for loved ones.
May the Love of God
fulfil His Purposes for them and in them all,
that in endurance or in healing,
in joy or in sorrow,
in new life in this world
or in welcoming to the greater New Life,
we all may be drawn to that fullness which is in Him alone.

Glory be to Our Father the All-loving,
glory be to Jesus
who came that we might have life in all its fullness,
glory be to the Holy Spirit
powerfully at work in our midst,
to the one God be glory for ever, Amen.

Celtic style

Prayer of invocation

This prayer is especially suitable for Christmas-time.

We call now on the Name of God,
The three-fold Trinity of Love,
On the Father who loves us,
On the Son who died and rose again,
On the Spirit who binds us together and empowers us.

Let us pray then, that the Holy Spirit,
which overshadowed Mary, may come upon us too,
that something of Christ
may be born afresh into this world through us.

*(Perhaps one might use a sung version of 'Veni Sancte Spiritus' or
'Come Holy Spirit' after each section.[1])*

May the Holy Spirit come upon us,
the Power of the Most High overshadow us,
so that through us too
something of Christ may come into this world.
CHORUS

May our earthly bodies, the body of this congregation,
become truly the Body of Christ,
filled with the Life that was in Christ.
CHORUS

May the earthly, everyday things
such as stables and mangers, offices and garages

---

1 'Veni Sancte Spiritus', *A Touching Place*, Wild Goose Publications, Glsagow, 1986
'Come Holy Spirit', *Enemy of Apathy*, Wild Goose Publications, Glasgow, 1988

be filled with a new glory
because of Jesus who was born in a manger and worked at a bench,
Jesus who now works through His children.
CHORUS

May people who work through the night,
such as shepherds and bus-drivers,
find a new glory in the midst of their busy lives,
through Him who comes to share every aspect of our lives.
CHORUS

May we, like Mary,
be blessed because we hear the Word of God and do it.
CHORUS

May we, like Mary, direct people in their hour of need to Jesus.
CHORUS

May we, like Mary, be still there in the darkness
when all that is good and godly seems to be dying.
CHORUS

May we, like Mary, live to see the triumph of life over death,
of love over hatred,
of God over human sin.
CHORUS

May we, like Joseph, be prepared to stand by quietly,
allowing others to be the centre of attention,
enabling others to fulfil their calling,
working in the background,
obedient to God and to none other.
CHORUS

Celtic style

Prayer of thanksgiving and homegoing

*An Alleluia could be sung after each 'we praise you' or this phrase
could be repeated as a response.*

Praise to You Our God,
Now we stand in the Glory of Your Love
to praise Your Holy Name,
Surrounded by 'the great cloud of witnesses unseen',
with the Apostles and Prophets,
we praise You.

With Mother Mary and the faithful women,
we praise You.

With Ninian, Columba, Bride
and all the faithful souls who followed them,
we praise You.

With all who have kept the light of the Gospel
burning down the ages, especially *(name them)*,
we praise You.

With all known to us who shared our earthly journey
and have reached Home before us,
we praise You.

For Your Peace flowing amongst us this night/day,
we Praise You.

For the healing of body, mind and soul
given through the Power of Your Word,
we praise You.

For the human instruments
through whom Your healing has been given,
we praise You.

The Love of God uphold you,
the Peace of God enfold you,
the Life of Jesus heal you,
the Word of Jesus lead you,
the Fire of the Spirit purify you.
the Wind of the Spirit drive you forward.
Have no fear.
The Lord is with you, not against you,
with you to protect you in danger,
with you to correct you when you go wrong.
God is Love, Father, Son and Holy Spirit,
One in love, in love for you,
this day and all eternity.

Prayers of guided silence

Introduction

This is another complete set of prayers with quite a different style using silence with only a minimum of comment. This method of prayer is, perhaps, most suitable for use in small groups in which people know each other.

For many people silence speaks louder than words, and it is in stillness that we *know* the Presence of God. A group using this type of prayer would usually go through the following stages: conversation and welcome; focus on the Word of God in Bible Study; silence and guided silence as suggested here.

This set of prayers outlines a use of silence in healing, and owes much to the Quaker tradition.

The length of pause between lines must be left to those who are leading the silence. The deeper the Fellowship of the Holy Spirit, the longer we can spend in silence, aware of the Presence.

For those who find silence difficult, it might be useful to fill in the gap with a Taizé-type chant, or with one of the quieter choruses, as suggested in the first prayer.

Guided silence

Prayer of approach

In this prayer, I include a possible use of the well-known chorus 'Be still and know'[1] adding a verse. Naturally, if one prefers to omit this and leave silences, one can do so.

In Name of the Father and of the Son and of the Holy Spirit, we gather.

We lift up our hearts to the God who says,
'Be still and know that I am God.' *(Ps. 46.10)*

Not in mental striving, nor in emotional feelings,
but in stillness let us seek to know His Presence.

Be still and know God as Our Father
welcoming and blessing his beloved sons and daughters.
(Sing verse 1 of 'Be still and know that I am God'.)

Be still and know Jesus moving silently through the midst of us.
(Sing verse 2 'I am the Lord who healeth thee'.)

Be still and open to the Holy Spirit who searches our hearts.
(Sing to the same tune 'Search me O God and know my heart'.[2])

Be still and know that I am God.
(Sing verse 3, 'In Thee O Lord I put my trust'.)

1 author unknown, *Songs and Hymns of Fellowship*, Kingsway Publications, Eastbourne, 1985.
2 This verse is not in the hymn books. I have inserted it to fit the prayer.

Guided silence

Prayer of confession

Jesus said, 'Whoever believes in me, out of his belly shall flow streams of living water'. *(John 7.38)*

If that healing flow is to go out from us,
we must make sure that nothing blocks it.

Let us open ourselves to God that all hindrances may be removed:
'Search me O God, and know me.
Try me and know my heart,
See if there is any wrong way in me.' *(Ps. 139)*

Are there any hurts or wrongs which we have not forgiven?
(silence)

Any possessions or status symbols of which we could not let go?
(silence)

Any relationships which need cleansing?
(silence)

Any weaknesses or failures which we have not been able to accept?
(silence)

Any lack of loving understanding in our midst here tonight/day
(silence)

The Lamb of God, who takes away the sin of the world,
lift from you the burden of these wrongs which you have faced,

Set you free to receive His Spirit
in whose power you can put things right,
And make you a vessel of His Healing Love.

Guided silence

Prayer for the healing of relationships

Jesus said, 'I am the Vine, you are the branches. Abide in me and let my words abide in you, so shall you bear much fruit. This is my command: love one another as I have loved you.' *(John 15.1)*

We abide in the Vine, when, like the branches of a vine,
we are all linked together in the one life which flows through us.

The Life-giving flow in the Vine which is Christ
is love for one another.
(silence)

From each one of us a whole network of relationships spreads out.
(silence)

Some are good and loving, so let us give thanks for those.
(silence)

Some, perhaps, need to be pruned, cut away, if we are to bear fruit.
(silence)

Some, perhaps, are broken and bruised,
and we need Christ's reconciling Love between us.
In Jesus' Name we face:

– possessiveness *(silence)*
– manipulative behaviour *(silence)*
– lust *(silence)*
– jealousy *(silence)*
in ourselves and in others.

Let us open ourselves to the redeeming Love of Christ in us
to set things right. *(silence)*

Where reconciliation is possible, show us the way, O Lord.
(silence)
Where no reconciliation is possible,
we surrender it all to You, the true Judge.

Some relationships have been broken by death,
yet in Christ we are still one,
and as we praise God we rise up to where they are.
'Holy Holy Holy, Lord God of Hosts,
heaven and earth are full of Your Glory,
glory be to you O Lord Most High.'

Let the network of relationships spreading out from us now
be alive with the Love of Christ. *(silence)*

Guided silence

Prayer of intercession

This prayer draws on Ephesians 3.18-20.

'Truly You Lord are in the midst of us and we are Your Family'

(silence)

May we know – truly know – with all God's people,
the breadth, the length, the depth and the height
of the Love of Christ.

(silence)

Into the depths of that love
let us bring the names of those in need,
dropping each name, so to speak,
into the depths of that love.

(silence – allow time for people to mention names, but not the nature of the trouble.)

From the depths of God's Love *(silence)*
To the heights of glory for which He created them *(silence)*
May these His beloved children be raised up with new life.

(silence)

In the all-enfolding breadth of the Love of God
Which goes to any length to reach us,
May these His beloved children be gathered up.

(silence)

Let them be filled, through all their being
with all the fullness of God.

(silence)

'Truly You Lord are in the midst of us and we are Your Family.'

Guided silence

Prayer of invocation

'I live, yet not I, but Christ liveth in me.' *(Galatians 2.20)*

So wrote the apostle Paul,
and so may it be true of us now.

We lay aside the merely human,
the self-made 'I' which intrudes upon and hinders
the work of the spirit.

Christ liveth in me *(silence)*
Christ *liveth* in me *(silence)*
Christ liveth in *me (silence)*

Christ in my looking *(silence)*
Christ in my listening *(silence)*
Christ in my touching *(silence)*
Christ in our togetherness *(silence)*

Christ in us meets the needs of those who come, not us,
For we have nothing to give them –
Only Christ in us.
Glory be to the Father and to the Son and to the Holy Spirit,
As it was in the beginning, is now and ever shall be,
World without end, Amen.

Guided silence

Prayer of thanksgiving and homegoing

There are a number of settings of Psalm 103.1, and most modern hymn books have at least one of them. One of these could be sung quietly.

'Rejoice in the Lord always, and again I say Rejoice!' *(Philippians 4.4)*
(silence)

Full of joy for what the Lord has been doing through us,
Let the light of joy shine out now.
(silence)

Bless the Lord O my soul, let all that is in me bless His Holy Name.
(Ps. 103.1)
(silence)

Bless the Lord, O my soul, and forget not all His Goodness.
(silence)

Let us now share with each other what the Lord has done for us.
(a time when people are free to speak to each other)

Bless the Lord, O my soul,
let all that is in me bless His Holy Name.
(silence)

Bless the Lord O my soul and forget not all His Goodness.

Glory be to the Father and to the Son and to the Holy Spirit,
As it was in the beginning, is now and ever shall be,
World without end, Amen.

Prayers and choruses

Introduction

Here are three acts of prayer which use choruses liturgically. There are advantages when such choruses are sufficiently well known to be sung without looking them up in the hymnbook.

Even if they have been so overused as to become hackneyed, yet they can still take on new value as part of a prayer which gives them new meaning.

I offer three examples here but I am aware that this is but a beginning!

Prayers and choruses

Prayer of approach

The Love of God

The following prayer, suitable for the beginning of a service, uses a well-known song,[1] and can be usually used without reference to hymnbooks. The music is to be found in Songs of God's People, number 26. Number 27, 'Father We Love You', could be used as an alternative. Both of these songs are in most modern hymnbooks.

Let us draw near to the mystery and wonder of the Love of God,
the Love of the Father over us,
the Love of Jesus sharing all things with us,
the Love of the Holy Spirit moving within us.
All is Love, all is One, and all is for us.

Let us pray:
Father, we Your Family come before You,
brothers and sisters in Your Love.
We, your quarrelsome, rebellious children gather before You,
hurt and unclean we seek to know Your Love for us afresh.
Abba, Father, behold Your Family. Father we adore you.

(Chorus)
'Father, we adore you,
Lay our lives before You,
How we love You.'

Jesus, we the disciples You have called gather before You,
we whose sins You have borne, whose pains You have known,
we whom You have empowered and sent into all the world,
Lord, we would know Your Presence now in our midst.

(Chorus)
'Jesus, we adore you,
Lay our lives before You,
How we love You.'

Holy Spirit, bearing witness within us
that we are indeed God's children,
kindle within us the burning fire of Love,
Love for God and for the Family of God.
Move us forward with the mighty Power of God
to save and to heal.
Holy Spirit forge the oneness
which may convince the world of the reality of the Gospel.
Spirit within us we adore you.

(Chorus)
'Spirit we adore You,
Lay our lives before You,
How we love You.'

Glory be to the Father and to the Son and to the Holy Spirit,
As it was in the beginning is now and ever shall be,
world without end, Amen.

(It might be a good idea to finish up with one of the many 'Alleluias'.)

Prayers and choruses

Prayer of approach

This is a prayer of approach where four different choruses can be used. They are often so well-known that no hymnbook is needed.

We draw near to the mystery of God,
the God who assures us that He loves us,
the God we doubt and disobey.
Yet however much we love or do not love God,
the love of God draws us now to Himself.
However much we doubt God,
He keeps faith with us.
However much we sin against His Love,
He keeps forgiving.

Let us now quietly and prayerfully call on God as Our Father,
using the very word Jesus used, the family word, 'Abba, Father'.

(chorus 'Abba, Father', no. 3 in Songs of God's People)

The love of God was lived out for *us* in Jesus of Nazareth,
Lived out to the full, lived to death and beyond it,
The love of God in Jesus is for us – for us tonight/today.

(chorus 'Jesus is Lord', verse 1 of no. 55 in Songs of God's People)

The love of God is in us now, moving through us,
Awakening us to new heights of living,
Forging us into an instrument of His Healing.

(chorus 'Spirit of the Living God', no. 98 in Songs of God's People)

O Love of God, Father, Son and Holy Spirit,
we open our hearts to you now.
Fill us with love for yourself and for each other,
and so may this service be real.
May words and music be alive with Your Love,
may our reaching out to each other
be a real sign of the Love of God.
May each of us contribute to the work of healing,
and each receive something of Your blessing,
through Jesus Christ Our Lord.

(hymn 'Father We Love You', no. 27 in Songs of God's People)

Prayers and choruses

The river of life

The following meditation can be used while the laying on of hands is being given, to keep the congregation prayerful, or alternatively it can be used as a time of healing without the laying on of hands. It is based on Ezekiel's vision, and uses the well-known song 'Peace is flowing like a river'[1] (no. 431 in Songs and Hymns of Fellowship) but I have slightly adapted it. Most books do not have the final 'Let it flow...' which is in Songs and Hymns of Fellowship. It can usually be sung without hymnbooks.

Jesus said, 'As the Father has loved me, so have I loved you, abide in my love.' *(John 15.9)*
Therefore His Love is now flowing out to us,
enfolding us, drawing us to Himself and to each other.

(chorus)
'Love is flowing like a river,
Flowing out to you and me,
Flowing out into the desert,
Setting all the captives free.'

Jesus said, 'Peace I leave with you, my peace I give you. Not peace as the world gives it, but my peace.' *(John 14.27)*
Therefore His Peace is now bathing us,
washing away fear, worry and ill-feeling.

(chorus)
'Peace is flowing like a river ...'

Jesus said, 'My Joy shall be in you, and your joy shall be full. Your joy shall no man take from you.' *(John 15.11 and 16.22)*

1 author unknown

Therefore His Joy is cascading out to us, shining and sparkling,
lighting us up, cleansing us of all that is dark and gloomy.

(chorus)
' Joy is flowing ...'

Jesus said, 'I am come so that you may have life and have it in all its
fullness.' *(John 10.10)*
'Because I live, you shall live also.' *(John 14.19)*
Therefore His Life is pouring out upon us, healing us, filling us,
raising us up to new heights.

(chorus)
'Life is flowing like a river ...'

Jesus said, 'As the Father sent me, so I now send you. Receive the
Holy Spirit. If a person believes in me, a stream of living water will
flow out of him'. *(John 7.38)*
Therefore His Love is flowing out from us
into the world around us,
bringing healing, new life and reconciliation.

Let it flow through me. Let it flow through me.
Let the mighty love of God flow through me. *(Repeat both lines.)*

Hymns

Introduction

Choosing hymns for a healing service is always problematic for there are so few hymns about healing in the usual hymnbooks. Therefore a little thought about this very important aspect of the service is in place.

The first thought is about hymnbooks themselves. People who are new to the church find it off-putting being being given several hymnbooks to manoeuvre on a narrow pew-shelf. If possible have the hymns printed out. Another point to consider is that if there are people present who are unwell or tense, hymns with a lot of verses can be a problem for them. We must either cut down the hymns to a couple of verses or else make it plain that one may sing sitting down. This, of course, is where choruses have the advantage.

There are not many problems involved in choosing the first and last hymns in the service. The first hymn should be one of praise, well known and easy to sing. Nothing is more off-putting than a weak start to a service because an unknown hymn is given out. Equally, the concluding hymn is easily chosen – dedication to Christ and thanksgiving for what He has done is expressed in so many hymns.

Now we come to think of the other hymns in the service. In this section I have used abbreviations for the hymnbooks. There is a guide on page 151 giving full details of all the hymnbooks mentioned.

There are some relevant hymns in *The Church Hymnary* Third Edition, with melody line – 'Thine arm O Lord' (CH3, 214) and 'At even when the sun was set' (CH3, 52), although some of the best verses from *The Revised Church Hymnary* are left out. Those in the section marked 'Healing' are weak.

There are two hymns in CH3 which are marked as being for children but which say more than some adult ones! These are numbers 426 and 427, both to well-known tunes.

'Jesus' Hands ...' (CH3, 228) is perhaps slightly too childish but makes a point. 'I feel the winds of God today' (CH3, 444) is very positive with a good tune, which also goes for an excellent hymn which was in the Revised Church Hymnary, 'The Lord is rich and merciful ...' (RCH, 398).

'How sweet the Name of Jesus sounds ... ' (CH3, 376) says a lot about inner healing, while 'Dear Lord and Father of mankind' (CH3, 76) helps to make us receptive, but beware the number of verses! – perhaps it is better sung seated. The same applies to 'Immortal Love ... ' (CH3, 306) and also to 'There's a wideness in God's mercy' (CH3, 218). The latter is also in *Mission Praise* as 'Souls of men ...' (MP, 559).

Another soothing, gentle song is 'Be still and know ...' (SHF, 37) in *Songs and Hymns of Fellowship* and so is 'Let the Son of God enfold you' (SHF, 403).

There is a beautiful hymn, 'Praise You, Lord ...' (MP, 541; SHF, 454) but not every congregation can cope with the rhythm. In *Mission Praise* there is a very good but little known hymn to a well-known hymn tune, 'Lord Thou hast given thyself for our healing' (MP, 243).

In *Songs of God's People* there are a number of suitable hymns: 'We cannot measure how you heal' (SGP, 112) and 'Christ's is the world ...' (SGP, 21). 'O Christ the Healer' (SGP, 82) is set to a well-known tune, and my own hymn 'Lifted high on Your Cross' (SGP, 66) links the Cross and healing.

In the following pages are three hymns which I have selected to end this hymn section.

Guide to Abbreviations

CH3   *Church Hymnary*, Third Edition, with melody line, Oxford University Press, 1973

RCH   *Revised Church Hymnary*, Oxford University Press, 1963

SGP   *Songs of God's People*, Oxford University Press, 1988

MP   *Mission Praise*, Marshall, Morgan and Scott, 1983

SHF   *Songs and Hymns of Fellowship*, Kingsway Publications, 1985

A hymn for the Christian Fellowship of Healing

This hymn is by my wife, Ailsa. It is a hymn of Invocation to the tune 'Woodlands' (CH3, 440; MP, 215).

We claim the Power of the Risen Son,
the Life fresh flowing from the Living God.
This was His prayer: that we should be as one,
alive with Christ and bonded by His Blood.

Creating Word, sustaining Lord is He.
And well He wrought us for His Loving Plans,
for we are nought, until we emptied be,
then are we all, filled by His Mighty Hands.

Only believe, believe as few would dare.
Trust in His Word with heart and mind and soul,
then will you know Whose company you share,
The Living Lord in whom all lives are whole!

We claim the Power of the Risen Son,
the Life fresh flowing from the Living God.
This was His prayer: that we should be as one,
alive with Christ and bonded by His Blood.

Come to Jesus

This hymn was written by the Rev. Irene Gillespie[1] to the Gaelic tune 'Chi mi Muile' ('I see Mull').

Come to Jesus, come to Jesus, come to Jesus and be healed. *(twice)*

Bring a broken heart that's bleeding,
bring a body racked with pain,
bring a mind and spirit needing
power to live and love again.

Come to Jesus, come to Jesus, come to Jesus and be healed. *(twice)*

Let Him place His Hands upon you
let Him set your spirit free,
let Him shower His Love upon you
as He did in Galilee.

Come to Jesus, come to Jesus, come to Jesus and be healed. *(twice)*

He will give His Peace for ever,
he will comfort and console,
keep His Promise that He'll never
leave His children less than whole.

Come to Jesus, come to Jesus, come to Jesus and be healed. *(twice)*

1 Used with permission.

Reconciliation

It is strangely difficult to find hymns about the healing of relationships. There is, of course, the hymn 'St Francis' Prayer' (SGP, 76), and 'We lay our broken world ... ' (SGP, 113) but there is very little anywhere about actually forgiving people who have wronged you, and who have caused suffering in the world. Yet this is at the heart of Jesus' teaching in the Sermon on the Mount, and at the heart of the Lord's prayer. As such it should have a place in a healing service and we should have hymns about it.

This has led me to write a hymn myself. The tune is an old Gaelic Communion hymn called 'The swan on the lake' sung with a long, slow swing as if rowing.

We stand in the dark at the foot of Your Cross,
the villains, their victims, the killers, the slain,
we're weary of warfare and sick with our loss,
O Lamb of God have mercy on us.

Enmeshed in the web of our anger and pain,
to Calvary's Hill we are drawn by Your Love,
to nail You afresh, and to pierce You again,
O Lamb of God have mercy on us.

Our sins and our hurts You now take as Your Own,
you bear all our sins and You share in our pain,
in love You are reaping the evil we've sown,
O Lamb of God have mercy on us.

We hear that great cry: 'O My Father forgive,
for they do not know what they do to You here'.
and so You are dying that we may all live,
O Lamb of God have mercy on us.

Forgiving each other as we've been forgiven,
we open our hearts and we cancel our debts,
and the Lord sets among us the Kingdom of Heaven,
the Lamb of God now gives us His peace.

Epilogue

I hope that this book will be of use to you, and that many will find healing of soul, mind and body through your ministry.

May the Spirit of the Lord Our God be upon you,
and anoint you to preach good news to the poor,
to heal the brokenhearted,
to proclaim liberty to the captives,
opening the prison for those who are bound,
to comfort those who mourn,
to give them beauty for ashes,
the oil of joy instead of mourning,
and to proclaim that the Kingdom of God
is here today,
open to all who will enter in.

To God be the glory,
to our Father,
to Jesus the Redeemer,
to the Holy Spirit powerfully at work within us,
One God, for ever Love, for ever One, for ever for us.

(adapted from Isaiah 61)

JESUS' HEALING WORKS AND OURS
Ian Cowie

Q. When is a miracle not a miracle?
A. When the supernatural is natural.

This is a book as much for those who have grown up with the stories of Jesus' miracles and now take them for granted as for those dismiss them along with Santa Claus and Peter Pan.

Ian Cowie re-translates the original Greek of the Gospels and sheds new light on what the healing miracles of Jesus were and what they mean for us. He concludes that there is no justification for saying that 'miracles' break the laws of nature, but that such events are a natural result of using untapped human and divine resources in a universe that is totally consistent.

In a very direct and informative way, the author carefully dissects the actions and words of Jesus in each healing incident and draws conclusions which are often at odds with current perceptions and interpretations.

This is possibly the first book to cover every single healing miracle of the New Testament, including those of the Apostles.

1 901557 27 8 · 256 pp · £9.99

PRAYING FOR THE DAWN
A Resource Book for the Ministry of Healing
Ruth Burgess & Kathy Galloway (eds)

The ministry of healing plays a vital and central part in the life of the Iona Community. It is a ministry in which justice is as important as medicine, reverence for the earth is as vital as respect for the individual person and the health of the body politic matters as much as the health of the body personal.

In addition to giving a taste of the background, context and range of this work, *Praying for the Dawn* offers detailed resources for those who wish to introduce the ministry of healing to their own churches or groups but are unsure of where to start. These guidelines, based on many years of experience of planning and leading services of prayer for healing and the laying-on of hands, both on Iona and elsewhere, are intended to give readers the confidence to go on and gain their own insights and experience in this work.

Includes several liturgies and a large section of worship resources – prayers, readings, meditations and blessings.

1 901557 26 X · 192 pp · £10.99

Visit our website at
www.ionabooks.com
for our full list of products and to order online

or contact us to request a catalogue:

Wild Goose Publications
Unit 16, Six Harmony Row
Glasgow G51 3BA, UK
Tel 0141 440 0985   Fax 0141 440 2338
e-mail: admin@wgp.iona.org.uk